The
Apostle
of Life

The Apostle of Life

Father Paul Marx, O.S.B.

Foreword by Claude Edward Newbury, MD
National President of Pro-Life
Johannesburg, South Africa

HUMAN LIFE INTERNATIONAL
7845 Airpark Rd., Suite E
Gaithersburg, Maryland 20879 USA
301/670-7884

HLI — CANADA, INC.
P.O. Box 7400, Station V
Vanier, Ontario K1L 8E4 CANADA
613/745-9405

Dedication

To you, our little "Freedom of Choice?" baby, I dedicate this book, for it is you above all who is exposing the real truth about abortion as the premeditated killing of living human beings. It is you who literally shows the world the torture inflicted on little souls by the abortionists. And you show it through hundreds of thousands of pictures printed and distributed in 97 countries thus far. I dedicate this book to you because you made the greatest sacrifice of all, you gave your life so that others may live.

TABLE OF CONTENTS

FOREWORD

T he *Special Reports* published by Father Paul
Marx, the founder of Human Life International, are
essential reading for persons involved in prolife
work. These reports reach remote areas of the world. They
are written mainly for Catholics, and they are often
disturbing because they confront readers with profound
questions about the fundamental issues of love, life, and
the family, and about the integrity and teaching of the
Catholic Church. These reports inform untold numbers of
people around the world, and they powerfully stimulate
individuals to defend Christian values. This educational
and stimulatory function is all the more important
nowadays because everywhere, almost without exception,
the public media are directly controlled by the enemies of
God, and their evil propaganda goes largely uncontested.
The Human Life International *Reports* provide essential
information that bypasses and restricts the malignant
influence of the public media.

Besides the news from America, the *Special Reports*
provide information gathered during Father Paul's
missionary journeys around the world. From this
knowledge, backed by his inspired intuition and enormous
experience, Father draws conclusions and suggests courses
of action and strategies to defeat those enemies of God who
work to kill unborn children by abortion and to kill the
handicapped and aged by euthanasia. The *Reports* provide
up-to-date information from prolife battlefronts in the
various parts of the world where Father has visited and
where he has established prolife organizations and agents.
I know of no other person who has amassed as much
experience—in the fields of abortion, infanticide,
euthanasia, population control, sex education,
demography, genetic engineering, fetal experimentation,
pornography, artificial birth control, and natural family
planning—as Father Marx.

Especially throughout the poverty-stricken "Third
World," Father has started, encouraged, and sustained

many prolife organizations. The poorly informed and powerless people of these countries are the main targets of the malice of the population-control lobby and the other sworn enemies of human life. Father Paul has observed and studied at firsthand most of the malevolent organizations, forces, and individuals that are assaulting the sanctity of human life. Their massive assault on humanity is now an unmistakable feature of society as we approach the end of the second millennium after the birth of Jesus Christ, and of His foundation of the Holy Catholic Church that He has guided and sustained throughout these last twenty centuries.

In these *Reports* Catholics, including the hierarchy, find their attention drawn often to the frightful and incontestable evidence of a great apostasy and rebellion that is now taking place in the Church.

Some readers dislike these *Reports* because, ostrich-like, they prefer to lower their heads in the pathetic hope that the beasts of prey who go about seeking to devour them and their families will fail to notice them, mistaking them for the other inanimate objects dotted about the veld. (Ironically, however, unlike many modern parents, ostriches—birds which the general public attributes small intelligence—will fearlessly attack those who seek to kill their offspring and will, by offering themselves as bait, lead predators away from their families.)

We live, thus, in times when many human parents kill their own unborn children for the sake of convenience, while ostriches, in common with other wild animals, are prepared to lay down their lives for their families.

Some years ago in South Africa, Father and I watched a single African buffalo fearlessly charge and rout two huge lionesses that were stalking the nearby herd of buffalo in the hope of singling out and killing a young buffalo. God gave us this unforgettable lesson to encourage us in our seemingly unequal fight against the powerful enemies of God. Jesus Our Lord tells us to pray without ceasing because the devil goes about like a roaring lion seeking to devour us. That fearless defense of the herd by a lone African buffalo reinforced the truth that direct physical action against our enemies will put them, also, to flight.

Many people imagine that by "playing possum" they will not be forced to face and confront the mortal enemies of God, life, love, and the family, who are thus the sworn enemies of the Catholic Church. They hope that because of this process of nonconfrontation the satanic enemies of God and man will politely go away, leaving them and their families in peace. Sadly, they fail to realize that an attack on one single human being, and an attack on the Catholic Church, is an attack on all mankind. It is so much more pleasant to spend one's life relaxing, "having a good day," and remaining undisturbed by the issues of abortion, infanticide, euthanasia, and the widespread devastation of morality, than to join the prolife crusade against those particular enemies of God, and His Church, who carry banners emblazoned with the armorial devices of the devil.

Few readers of Father Paul's *Reports* will cling to any doubt about the diabolical nature of the worldwide antilife conspiracy. It takes faith and courage to fight against the enemies of life, as those who are motivated to action by Father's *Reports* will soon discover. They will also discover that this endeavor entails a direct, almost tangible, contact with the God who most bountifully sustains His friends. Those who deliberately neglect their God-given duty to join the struggle against the antilife forces are imperiling their own lives and the lives of their children and grandchildren. Worse still, if they fail to join the crusade they miss the opportunity of being blessed with the torrent of grace that God especially gives to those engaged in prolife work.

Readers of these *Reports* are forced to examine, and then to confront, the widespread evil in the modern world. More sadly still, they must face the dreadful and incontestable evidence of widespread heresy and apostasy within the Catholic Church, as recounted in almost every issue. This autodemolition of the Catholic Church is the real horror, for the survival of mankind depends on the Church. When the Church is strong, the world's moral climate improves and civilization flourishes; but when the Church is weak, the fearful and eternal enemies of Christ are unleashed to inflict their evil, almost without impediment. Should the light of the Catholic faith grow dim, the whole world would plunge into moral darkness, as the enemies of God and His Church know full well. That is why they have concentrated their diabolical efforts in attacks on the Catholic Church, both from without and from within. To use the apocalyptic words of Pope Paul Vl, "The smoke of Satan has penetrated the sanctuary of God."

Father Paul's *Reports* are always inspiring, filled as they are with the living evidence of the truth, strength, and beauty of Catholic orthodoxy and of the faith, courage, love, and vitality of countless Catholics and non-Catholics around the world. These *Reports* often provide shocking news about the scandalous behavior of many Catholic bishops, priests, and religious and civic leaders. Some of these *Reports* might be viewed with incredulity by uninformed readers who try to avert their gaze from the dreadful evidence of the worldwide destruction of morals and the sad situation within the Catholic Church, which Father Paul so lucidly and fearlessly documents. Some of the information is appalling in its revelation of the cowardice, perversions, and defiance of the authority of Christ and His Vicar the Pope, by many Catholic bishops, priests, theologians, and religious.

The following conditions prevail in many (not all!) dioceses of the Catholic Church today.

1. The bishops and clergy are no longer teaching the traditional doctrines of the Church, in particular those contained in *Humanae Vitae,* and are tolerating their congregation's disregard of these doctrines.

2. The bishops and clergy are no longer credibly fighting the menace of abortion, euthanasia, pornography, divorce, fornication, and permissiveness and are thus creating the impression that the Catholic Church will condone these evils under certain circumstances.

3. The bishops and clergy are, sometimes deliberately and sometimes subconsciously, undermining the authority of the pope.

4. The bishops in many areas of the world, especially in those with a Western culture, are allowing theologians to destroy the traditional teaching of the Catholic Church and to directly contradict the authority of the pope, sometimes even defending and protecting these theologians.

5. There is concrete evidence of immorality practiced by members of the Catholic clergy themselves, which the bishops either disregard or deal with in a totally unsatisfactory manner.

6. Many bishops and clergy are now actively engaged in persecuting Catholics who resist the widespread abuses and the heresy of Modernism in the Church.

7. Many bishops are condoning gravely sinful behavior in seminaries, including fornication and sodomy among seminarians and staff members, and are tolerating the teaching of heresies to students.

The above-mentioned conditions are causing a scandal of immense proportions among Catholics. Many of them are leaving the Catholic Church to join Protestant churches that still adhere to traditional Christian teaching and will not tolerate the scandal of immorality by their pastors. Many others, through total disillusionment, are ceasing to practice any form of religion at all.

These conditions are, possibly, worse than those that prevailed in the Catholic Church at the time of the Reformation. Had the Catholic hierarchy taken appropriate remedial and disciplinary action at that time, the calamity of the Reformation could have been averted and the faith of millions could have been saved.

Parallel with the betrayal of Christ and His Church, Father Paul presents many accounts of the great courage and faith displayed by many faithful Catholic priests, bishops, and religious.

Father and his thirty-eight committed associates across the world have poured vast quantities of prolife educational and religious material into many countries, including my own, South Africa. Father has also subsidized the attendance of people from around the world at his international conferences on love, life, and the family. With his help, and that of his generous benefactors (mainly Americans), we have been able in South Africa to defeat demands for abortion-on-request on three separate occasions during the last eight years—the last call coming as recently as 1990—and to turn away the demands for euthanasia. With his help, we have also been able to delay the introduction of pagan sex-education materials into our

state-subsidized schools, to retard seriously the population-control lobby, and to hamstring the pornographers.
It is only now that these pagan sex-education programs
are beginning to make their way into the schools, assisted
and motivated by Planned Parenthood—that ubiquitous
mortal enemy of God, His Catholic Church, and all
mankind—and accompanied by impassioned cries that
children must be educated in the techniques of sexual
intercourse, in sexual perversions, and in the use of
condoms, in order to slow down the genocidal AIDS
epidemic now raging in Africa.

At present (September 1991), Father, in association with
the two branches of Human Life International that he has
established and sustained in South Africa, is helping the
people of Botswana attempt to defeat a call for abortion in
the parliament of that rich, vast, and sparsely populated
country. Like a modern St. Paul, he has worked in 84
countries and shipped prolife materials to 111. No wonder
Pope John Paul recently called him "The Apostle of Life"!

There is no doubt whatsoever that the enemies of God
have inflicted mortal damage on civilization through
abortion, infanticide, euthanasia, and the gateway to it all,
contraception. That is why the prolife movement is so
important in the struggle to preserve civilization. If the
enemies of life are able to deceive society into accepting the
killing of unborn children as a "reproductive right," then at
one fell stroke they will have gained a great strategic
advantage in the battle to destroy all morality. Once any
nation comes to accept the killing of unborn children, it
thereby discounts God and His commandments and
devalues all human life, and inevitably all morality;
consequently, its civilization will rapidly decline and
disasters will overtake that nation. God will turn His face
away from it and fearfully punish it. That is one reason the
outcome of the prolife struggle is so important.

St. Benedict of Nursia and his monks, down through
the ages, have preserved the Catholic Faith and have
created and encouraged conditions that in earlier times
preserved civilization when barbarian hordes overran the
world. The Benedictines were largely instrumental in
prompting a Christian civilization to flower, nourished by

the principles of Roman Catholicism. The climate of charity, faith, and hope that emanated from Benedictine monasteries, and their preservation of learning, arts, crafts, agriculture, and culture allowed.mankind to break free from the twofold darkness of sin and ignorance into which it had sunk.

In our times a disciple of St. Benedict, Father Paul Marx, in following faithfully the example of the many Benedictine saints among whom is counted the illustrious reformer of the Church, St. Gregory the Great, has been immensely influential in the battle to preserve civilization by preserving the Catholic Faith.

Those who are fortunate enough to receive these compelling and disturbing newsletters invariably pass them on to others, often wishing later that these jewels of Catholic truth and morality were still in their possession for future meditation and reference. The inestimably valuable information they contain—and their insights into the working of the modern world and the networking of the forces of evil—make these monthly letters unique. So it is a great blessing that many of the articles published in these newsletters throughout the year are collected, edited, and published as a compendium. Father is truly a prolife missionary and visionary to the whole world.

Human Life International, under his inspired leadership, fulfills a vital function in the Catholic Church. It continually draws the attention of the hierarchy to the abuses and evils in the Church and the world. It also furnishes enough details of these dangers to enable the hierarchy to act against them if they wish. Only if the admonitions of people like Father Paul are heeded without delay by Catholics, and especially by the Catholic clergy and hierarchy, can the world avert the abysmal calamity of a second "reformation" and a new barbarian age.

Claude Edward Newbury, MD
National President of Pro-Life
Johannesburg, South Africa
16 September 1991

INTRODUCTION

"Be on your way, and remember:
I am sending you as lambs in the midst of wolves."
Luke 10:3

Ten years ago, after having spent over thirty years of my priestly life opposing the antilife propaganda of the International Planned Parenthood Federation, Planned Parenthood of America, various United Nations agencies (like UNICEF and UNESCO), and other international prodeath organizations, I knew the time had come to form a prolife organization that would go into every country in the world to fight these forces of death. The organization I formed and the banner we fight under is Human Life International.

On this tenth anniversary of HLI we have put together this special book, *The Apostle of Life*, for all who engage in pro-life/pro-family work. The book is special for three reasons: It chronicles HLI's dramatic work over the past ten months to fight the forces of death throughout the world. It is my annual report to all HLI "shareholders" and other prolife workers. It is also an account highlighting HLI's goals, effectiveness, and growth over the past decade.

It is critical that you read this book. The fight for life is the most vital cause in which you can possibly engage. I am sure that is why, during one of my meetings with Pope John Paul II, he looked me in the eyes and said, "You are doing the most important work on earth." And then, this past summer, at another meeting with the Holy Father, he called me **"The Apostle of Life."** That explains the title of this book.

The pope knows, as few others do, that in today's rapidly changing world, with the collapse of Communism and the breakup of the Soviet Union, a leadership vacuum is being created. The Holy Father looks on all this change as the Church's opportunity to fill that vacuum with God's message of hope and love and life. The atheistic Communist system must not be replaced by another godless one.

You and I, through the work of Human Life International, are helping the Holy Father in this tremendous re-evangelization of the world. The first and most critical step in this glorious work is to bring man to see the sanctity of life, all life—from womb to tomb—because all life is precious to God. That is the task of Human Life International, a task you share in so intimately.

Through the pages of this book you will be encouraged and inspired to maintain your opposition to the demonic plans of worldwide death agencies like Planned Parenthood, NARAL, NOW, the Hemlock Society, the Right to Die Society, many U.S. government-sponsored groups like the U.S. Agency for International Development, and even international governing bodies like the United Nations. Your commitment to see this fight through to victory is critical. No matter how tired we get in our work, no matter how small the victories, no matter how vicious the attacks launched against us, we must run the race to the end. As Mother Teresa tells us, "We are not called to be successful; we are called to be faithful." At times, that is very difficult.

Not a day goes by that our message of life and love is not attacked and ridiculed by the news and entertainment media. TV shows, newspapers, news broadcasts, movies, and secular books and magazines all promote the propaganda and lies of the abortionists and the sellers of death while denying the sanctity of life.

They tell you that your elderly father crippled with arthritis or debilitated by Parkinson's should be saved from his misery and peacefully "put to sleep"; so, too, with your aging mother who has Alzheimer's or a painful bone cancer. If you truly love your parents, these "angels of death" tell you, then kill them yourself, or at least give them the means to end their misery. Let them die with dignity. Such thinking has spread so rapidly that this November the people of Washington State will vote on whether or not to pass ballot initiative 119, which would give doctors the right to kill their patients. Incredibly, author Derek Humphrey's how-to suicide manual, *The Final Exit,* is a best-seller and has even been printed in extra large type. Even the American Medical Association has done away with its Hippocratic Oath. Mind you, all this killing is performed in the name of "love and mercy."

But this isn't love, and it certainly isn't merciful. These death merchants proudly interfere with God's will. Even though we cannot fully understand all the human suffering that goes on in the world, we can trust in God that whatever happens to us or to our loved ones is for our best. And we know that God, Lover that He is, will turn into eternal happiness and joy whatever temporary pain and suffering any one of us or any one of our loved ones must endure in this lifetime.

The merchants of death preach the so-called quality of life. An infant child born with spina bifida or a young woman thrust into a coma from a car accident or a middle-aged man paralyzed after a stroke—since these people have no chance of leading "normal" lives, they should be starved to death. In this way, they would not become a "burden" to society. In other words, a person is valuable to society not because he *is* but because of what he *can do.* What is this reasoning but one more in a series of denials of God's supremacy to rule over His own creation?

Then there is the horror of abortion. Abortion is the most selfish and abhorrent crime committed by man for two reasons: (1) its victims are so innocent and defenseless, and (2) the crime is so terribly brutal.

What's more, there is no more callous denial of God's Being than abortion. In abortion, man sets himself up as God to decide who shall live and who shall die. But man deserves no such power, for the simple reason that man does not create himself. To think otherwise is to deny God His true Being as the Author of Life.

The contraceptive mentality goes hand in glove with abortion. Contraception, too, is the denial of God as the Author of Life, because when man uses contraceptives he again makes himself the determinant of who shall live and who shall not. Contraception is the clearest symbol of man's putting a barrier between himself and his God, because it literally puts a barrier between man and life. And God is Life. When man denies the possibility of life, he denies the reality of life.

As serious as this media antilife preaching is, a far more sinister evil faces all of us in the prolife movement. This evil comes from within the Catholic Church itself. I cannot begin to list for you all the bishops around the world who actively preach against *Humanae Vitae* and the Church's teachings on the sanctity of life (you will come across many in the chapters of this book). There is so much apostasy that many of the world's Catholics resemble sheep without shepherds. Today's bishops have failed to heed the warning of the late Bishop Sheen: "Whenever the Church marries an age, She finds Herself a widow in the next one." This rebellion within the Church makes the Holy Father's work even more difficult.

That is why those of us loyal to the Holy Father and dedicated to the life principles of Holy Mother Church must redouble our efforts and join Pope John Paul II in his work of re-evangelizing the world. That is exactly what you do when you support Human Life International. Through the pages of this book you will come to know of the tremendous commitment of your fellow workers in God's prolife vineyard. Although the Holy Father called me The Apostle of Life, there are, of course, many other apostles throughout the world. Some you'll read about are:

Cardinal Hans Herman Groer, Archbishop Georg Eder, Bishop Klaus Küng, and Bishop Kurt Krenn—all from Austria. In the face of fierce and vicious opposition from theologians and so-called Catholic newspapers, these courageous bishops retracted Austria's dissent to *Humanae Vitae*. These are true apostles.

The prolife crisis in Eastern Europe is staggering. But there is hope, as can be seen by the fact that over 600 doctors, health workers, and leaders from fifteen countries attended our historic prolife conference in Slavonski Brod, Yugoslavia. To stage such an event would have been impossible even five years ago. I spoke at the conference. From past meetings there I had learned of a young, active surgeon, Antun Lisec, who today spends all his time traveling through Yugoslavia and neighboring countries

showing prolife films, holding conferences, and counseling women against abortion. He is an Apostle of Life on
our payroll.

Last fall our co-sponsored symposium in Bratislava,
Czechoslovakia, drew 1,500 participants from Eastern
Europe. More than 400 attended our seminars in Poland
and Lithuania. All these attendees have the potential to
become Apostles for Life.

Gisela Kohler, a mother of six, began East Germany's
young prolife movement with the endorsement of just one
priest. Today she has collected 42,000 signatures of people
who oppose abortion. Gisela is another Apostle of Life.

Dr. Siegfried Ernst of Germany, the recipient of the
1991 International Human Life Award, gave a tremendous
defense of *Humanae Vitae* that HLI printed as a booklet
entitled "Is *Humanae Vitae* Outdated?" and sent to bishops
all over the world. It is ironic that Dr. Ernst, a Lutheran,
would be affirming to Catholic bishops in North America
and Europe the truths contained in *HV!* Dr. Ernst is yet
another Apostle of Life.

In Latin America many thousands work very hard to
join the Church's work. Dr. Edgardo Llanos and Astrida de
Bayer are doing tremendous work in Barranquilla and
Bogotá, Colombia. In spite of death threats, Cardinal
Lopez Trujillo of Medellin, Colombia, continues to speak
out strongly against contraception and abortion, now as
president of the Pontifical Council for the Family. Three
more Apostles of Life!

When Bishop Quinn of Sacramento, California, turned
his cathedral over for part of the inauguration ceremonies
for California's newly elected pro-abortion Governor, Pete
Wilson, eleven apostles stepped forward to protest this
outrage: Joe Scheidler, Jack Cook, Charles Shunk, Nell
Keim, Dr. John Byrnes and his brother Michael, Scott
Kiley, Al Rhomberg, and Richard Szabo and his sister,
Theresa. Tragically, the eleventh apostle, 81-year-old John
Szabo, died several weeks after being physically removed
from Bishop Quinn's cathedral. His daughter attributes his
death to the trauma he underwent during his stand for
life. John Szabo died for his faith. He is an Apostle and
Martyr for Life.

Bede Perera works tirelessly every day in Sri Lanka, as do Dr. and Mrs. Claude Newbury in South Africa, Sister Pilar Versoza in the Philippines, and many, many others elsewhere around the world. These are just a few of the apostles you will read about in this book. They are our people, and we are proud of them.

In addition, there are literally tens of thousands of individuals like you who are also Apostles of Life and help make all of HLI's work possible.

When the Lithuanian seminarian Robertas Skrinkas wrote HLI and asked us to send him prolife materials for his fellow students, your contributions helped us supply his need. When our full-time prolife apostle in Africa, Lawrence Adekoya, called and asked HLI to send him two new copies of "The Silent Scream" because his old ones were literally worn out from having been shown so many times, your contributions helped pay the $990 to buy and ship him the films. With the $22,000 Toyota jeep you helped buy for him, Lawrence roams through Nigeria bringing the prolife/pro-family message to many thousands. When the HLI Latin America head Magaly Llaguno budgeted $160,000 for her Miami office to purchase and send videos, films, and literature to crisis spots in South and Central America, your contributions helped us give her the needed funds. When young prolife leaders from around the world, like Carlos Polo from Peru, asked us for help so they could attend our HLI world conferences on love, life, and the family, your contributions helped bring those leaders to our conferences. (After attending our conferences, Carlos went home and played a major role in stopping the legalization of abortion in Peru!) Our man in Costa Rica, Eduardo Loria, also attended the California conference, went home, and became the chief influence in defeating the introduction of a Planned Parenthood sex-education course in the schools.

Those are just some of the ways your prayers and contributions have helped HLI Apostles of Life do their work. So as you read through this book and journey with me over the past ten years of Human Life International, know that you, too, are here in this book. In a sense, you are the binding that holds the pages together because you help supply HLI with the resources—both spiritual and financial—we so desperately need in order for our work to succeed and bear fruit. I pray that God will richly bless you for the help you have already given HLI, and I hope this annual report inspires You to continue to join me and all the other Apostles of Life at work among our thirty-eight international branches as we do what the Holy Father calls the most important work on earth.

Paul Marx, OSB, Ph.D.

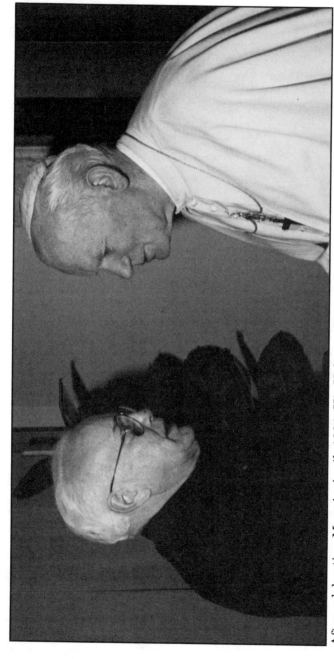

After celebrating Mass in April, 1991, His Holiness Pope John Paul II called Father Marx "The Apostle of Life."

Inside Europe

No. 74   November 1990

I've reported to you several times on the religious
situation in Austria, a country slightly smaller than
Maine, with seven million people, where each year
85,000 babies are born and 100,000 killed. In 1974 I covered
the country in a prolife speaking tour. Later that year
parliament gutted the law protecting preborn children.

Recently I revisited Austria to shore up our prolife
friends and forces. Sixteen prolife films, ten of which our
benefactors generously paid for, are being shown throughout the country right now.

BISHOPS ADMIT THEIR ERROR

To improve the appalling condition of the Austrian
Catholic Church, Pope John Paul II in the last few years
has appointed several good bishops: Cardinal Hans
Herman Groer, a Benedictine monk and national head of
the Legion of Mary, for Vienna; Archbishop Georg Eder, a
pastor, for Salzburg; Klaus Küng, an Opus Dei priest, for
Feldkirch; and Kurt Krenn, a brilliant young theologian,
as auxiliary bishop of Vienna in charge of science, art, and
culture. Rebellious priests, theologians, and leading laymen vigorously protested all of these appointments,
especially those of Bishops Eder, Krenn, and Küng. But
the pope stood firm.

About two years ago the Austrian hierarchy, at the
request of His Holiness and with the mediation of Bishop
Krenn, retracted its dissent to *Humanae Vitae*. Austria's
Catholic press was so shocked over this retraction that for

---

*About two years ago the Austrian
hierarchy retracted its dissent to
Humanae Vitae.*

---

a long time it refused to publish it. Nor was it published in
the USA until HLI did so; we also gave it to *The Wanderer*,
which then printed it. Twice we sent the story to the U.S.
bishops' National Catholic News Service, which suppressed

it. In Austria, no bishops have publicized the story except those appointed recently, and even they have not done much, except for Bishop Krenn.

"CATHOLIC" OFFICIALS PUSH CONTRACEPTION & ABORTIFACIENTS

Totally ignoring the reversal of the dissent was the powerful archdiocesan Institut für Ehe und Familie (Institute for Marriage and Family) in Vienna. The institute serves the whole country and publishes *Ich Du Wir (I You We)*, a substantial booklet with the subtitle "Information about Family Planning as a Foundation for Responsible Parenthood." This pro-contraception booklet is given to every engaged couple in Austria; 180,000 have been printed.

One of the advisors for the *Ich Du Wir (IDW)* was Austria's own version of Father Richard McCormick, his fellow Jesuit Hans Rotter, professor of moral theology at the University of Innsbruck. Among the advisors were Pill enthusiasts such as the leading gynecologist Andreas Seidl and the master of theology Helmut Schüller, also director of the powerful Caritas charitable organization in Vienna.

IDW gives a detailed explanation of all birth-"control" methods and of the reproductive system. Strangely, it fails to mention the abortifacient character of the Pill specifically and directly, even though all three functions of the Pill—contraceptive, sterilizing, and abortifacient—have been condemned by the Church for twenty centuries.

IDW asserts that "Die 'Pille' ist ein Medikament." But it's not! Fertility is not a disease. Pregnancy is not an illness. *IDW* lists the Pill's side effects (that is, its unwanted effects) rather well but says nothing about the injectible Depo-Provera's being so dangerous that it's forbidden to U.S. women, or about its abortifacient character. The document *does* admit, without amplification, that the IUD and "die Pille danach" (the morning-after Pill) prevent implantation.

In discussing conscience, *IDW* never really makes clear that a well-formed conscience excludes contraception. Sterilization is described in detail but, again, the reader is not told what the Church has always taught: direct sterilization is intrinsically immoral. *IDW* merely records that the state allows sterilization after one's twenty-fifth year.

The document mentions the Austrian bishops' dissent but barely mentions their retraction of it. It totally ignores Pope John Paul II's repeated insistence that *Humanae Vitae* is not debatable theologically, because the matter is settled.

IDW is a typical product of double-talking theologians and their cohorts, who even at this late date don't see the mess caused by their dissenting teachings. Meanwhile, two bishops have appealed to the Sacred Congregation for the Doctrine of the Faith concerning the false teaching in this key treatise for engaged Catholics.

BISHOPS & ABORTION

The Benedictine Cardinal Groer is a very pious man. But more and more girls are serving Mass; to tell them not to serve would "scar them emotionally for life," says the cardinal. He hasn't condemned the practice.

Abortion was the biggest issue in the recent national election campaign. One of the chief reasons is the untiring activity of HLI's great friend, Martin Humer, over the years. He recently founded the Christian Voters' Party, which may have a chance of success.

Because the shrill feminists and their sympathizers accuse the Church of wanting to punish women, Cardinal Groer says there should be no legal penalty for mothers who have their unborn babies killed. But he recently stated what Humer has said for years, that the law should punish abortionists and fathers. This statement blew up a storm of protest from the media.

Except for Cardinal Groer and Bishop Krenn, the Austrian bishops aren't noted for actively opposing abortion. Not even Cardinal Groer has strongly called for changing or abolishing the abortion-on-demand law. He says he's waiting for, and working for, a change of conscience. But doesn't law educate, restrain, and remind?

Austria produces more abortions than births, more

coffins than cradles. After Germany, she's the fastest-dying nation on earth. No one cares to venture how many foreigners, and among them how many Moslems, live in this picture-postcard country. There are a huge mosque and many Moslem "prayer houses" in once-Catholic Vienna. Austria's prostitution, pornography, and sex "education" are frightening.

One Viennese pastor told me only 3 percent of his parishioners attend Sunday Mass regularly, but he estimated that maybe 10 percent of all Viennese do. The whole country ordained only fifty-six priests this year. Hundreds of priests from Poland are filling in the gaps and plugging the holes. But then, old people are dying off fast, and the comparatively few young people don't learn their faith in the schools. Meanwhile, Jehovah's Witnesses and other sects are very active.

TAX-PAID PORNOGRAGHY

The Socialist government has inflicted one of the worst Planned Parenthood-type sex-"education" programs on the school children. PP has no formal organization in Austria but seems to work through the corrupt government.

Only recently the government spread *AIDS—Ratgeber für Alle (AIDS: Advice for All)* nationwide. In it the condom is king, of course; the little illustrations, embarrassingly pornographic, seem calculated to foster a sexual ethic pleasing to hedonists and homosexuals. Austrian Catholics are waiting for their bishops to condemn this condom-happy document.

The chief means of birth "control" are the Pill, surgical abortion, and, increasingly, sterilization. "Catholic" doctors

---

One great light in Austria is the heroic work of Austria's great natural family planning authority, Dr. Josef Rötzer.

---

consistently tell both married and engaged couples to use "die anti-Baby Pille" after they have two children. One great light in Austria is the heroic work of Austria's great natural family planning (NFP) authority, Dr. Josef Rötzer, whose basic text has gone through nineteen editions. Recently the Holy See named him a Knight of St. Gregory.

Because of the dwindling number of Catholics, the aging of the nation, and the bishops' need for more and more money to keep their schools going, last spring the prelates launched a three-year, $3.3 million TV advertising campaign to persuade Catholics to really support the Church. Alas, "Teach your people to pray, and they will pay," as my pastoral-theology professor said forty-five years ago.

HISTORIC PROLIFE CONFERENCE IN SLAVONSKI BROD

This meeting in Yugoslavia for medical personnel and leaders of Eastern Europe, cosponsored by HLI and the World Federation of Doctors Who Respect Human Life, was a smashing success. Our friends' generosity paid most of the expenses. More than 600 doctors, health workers, and leaders from fifteen countries attended. I addressed them on abortion, euthanasia, and feminism.

I wish I had room to summarize the forty excellent talks, including those by people from countries now recovering from the trauma of Communism. One Croatian research doctor reported on the unbelievable ignorance of Croatian women concerning preborn children. They've heard nothing but proabortion lies for forty-five years.

I was particularly impressed by the thirty-five people, mostly doctors, who came from Lithuania. Besides attending daily Mass, they edifyingly prayed together at other times. How sick they are of Communism, and how much they want to be rid of Soviet occupation!

In Eastern Europe the abortion holocaust, the religious conditions, the economic stagnation, the environmental crises, and the low birthrates are far worse than I've reported to you so far. For example, the five million Catholic Croatians officially report more than 35,000 abortions, and the number of unofficial ones could be double or triple that!

Ethnically fragmented Yugoslavia's twenty-three million inhabitants may commit 800,000 baby killings annually. No wonder, as one doctor reported, that infertility treatment is a problem and only 8 percent successful. Women talk about having had five or ten abortions. "Often they don't know whether to cry or to be angry," a woman doctor reported. Many more young Yugoslavs are aborted than are born.

Poorly paid to begin with, most gynecologists cannot make a living unless they perform abortions. One cardinal said he knew a woman who had had thirty-three abortions. Nature, being jealous of her fertility, often arranges ovulation within two or three weeks after an abortion. Present at our conference were doctors who were still performing abortions. One abortionist always baptized the babies he was about to kill!

THE CASE OF THE DISAPPEARING VILLAGES

Whole areas and villages are dying out in Yugoslavia. Some 25 percent of all Yugoslavs are unemployed, with prices high and inflation almost out of control. With Blessed Mary's help, the two most prosperous Catholic republics of Croatia and Slovenia have voted the hated Communists out. But the 500,000 militant Serbs who live in Croatia are creating problems. The four poorer, Eastern Orthodox republics are trying to beat Communism with elections.

Many Yugoslavs have left the country, 600,000 (mostly Croatians) having gone to Germany. The nation is aging fast, and the government is loath to allow further emigration, falsely asserting that the collapse of the birthrate is due to young people's leaving. The political situation is extremely unstable; civil war may come.

Meanwhile, the four million Moslems are quietly plotting, praying in their mosques and prayer centers, and multiplying. They're working their way into the larger society, wielding ever more power and making increasing demands. The eight million militantly nationalistic, Orthodox Serbs, who don't go to church much, are at wits' end about how to control the proud, autonomous territory of Kosovo, which is already 80 percent Moslem, mostly ethnic Albanians.

The full-color printing press our supporters bought for our branch in Slavonski Brod, under the great Father Marko Majstorovic, is grinding out mountains of prolife/ profamily and catechetical literature for Yugoslavia and neighboring countries. On September 19-21 our branch in Zagreb sponsored a much-needed symposium on marriage preparation. Father Matthew Habiger, OSB, of St. Benedict's College in Atchison, Kansas, stood in for me. He spoke on NFP and *Humanae Vitae* as integral parts of marriage preparation. (Father Habiger will join HLI in January.)

H.L.I. AIDS SLOVAK & HUNGARIAN PROLIFERS

In Bratislava, Slovakia, we're planning a national prolife/ profamily seminar for medical personnel in the largest hall in town at the end of April. We'll do a similar program in Budapest, Hungary, and then one in Vilnius, Lithuania. Our pictures of aborted babies have been extremely effective in these countries, by the way.

Prolifers won an enormous victory in Slovakia: Dr. Vladimir Krcmery of the Slovakian Department of Health Services reports that nurses, gynecologists, and other doctors who refuse to perform abortions or take part in them will no longer be punished or discriminated against. Our opportunities to save babies in Eastern Europe are mind-boggling. We'd despair without the prayers and generosity of our dear friends.

In once-Catholic Hungary, to which we've already begun sending much literature and many audiovisual aids, three abortions are still induced for every live birth. Dr. Andras Szorenyi, the Bernard Nathanson of Hungary, wants to work closely with us to save babies in every way possible.

With tears, great humility, and touching frankness he told me personally how he had betrayed his medical ethics and how many little ones he had killed. Now he wants to make amends, and he will, with your prayers. We both felt like crying over the millions of babies who've been killed, but instead we began laying plans for my mission journey to Hungary next May. We've already shipped key literature to Dr. Szorenyi.

Hungary reports 90,000 abortions for ten million people, but the true death figure is surely much higher. The country registers more funerals than births. This dying nation is aging fast. Today 340,000 fewer Hungarians exist than in 1980! Some 2.4 million people live on pension. Doctors behind the crumbled curtain are putting HLI's pictures of aborted babies in their offices. (Can you imagine U.S. and Canadian doctors doing that?)

Is there any end to the wickedness of the wealthy International Planned Parenthood Federation (IPPF), with its 113 national affiliates and hundreds of branches? Dr. Janos Foldenyi of the Hungarian Ministry of Health told me that IPPF sent medical doctors to train Romanians to perform abortions in that country, after their govern-ment fell last December. IPPF also dumped tons of contraceptives and abortifacients on poor Romania.

And now the secretary general of IPPF has written to Hungary's premier, Joszef Antall, offering condoms and abortifacient Pills and IUDs below cost, in any quantity desired. Dr. Foldenyi says the premier has no idea what IPPF is, or how its programs destroy youth and family.

He wants HLI and other groups to write to Premier Antall to warn him about IPPF. The premier and Cardinal Jean-Marie Lustiger of Paris recently discussed the situation of the Catholic Church in Hungary, the heroic Cardinal Mindszenty's historical role, and the gigantic tasks of regenerating Catholic education and "restoring the prestige of the Churches."

A PEEK INSIDE THE EVIL EMPIRE

I learned much about the USSR from people at our Yugoslav conference. The Soviet empire is in religious, economic, and social chaos. So disorganized is the Red "paradise" that its current record harvest lies rotting in the fields or spoiling in warehouses. The old-fashioned oil-pumping system cannot take advantage of present opportunities.

All are hungry; many are starving. Alcoholism presents a gigantic problem. Religious literature is minimal. Abortions outnumber births two to one. The sixty-five million Moslems increase and multiply.

Even the Orthodox and Uniate (Catholic) Churches are in conflict. The Uniates are getting back more and more churches that the Reds had given to the Russian Orthodox Church. Whole villages are demanding the return of their churches. They're seeking functioning pastors, but the priests are far too few. There are many vocations, thank God. And a goodly number of priests from the Orthodox Church are joining the Uniate Church.

Just think: if the Catholic Church hadn't collapsed in the West, thousands of missionaries could now go into the USSR and bring the Good News to 280 million religion starved people who at last have attained freedom to worship openly and to spread their faith.

Poland, the only source of missionaries in the West today, has been quietly preparing for this day. A Polish bishop and several priests and nuns have gone into the USSR to evangelize. The Catholic University at Lublin, where Pope John Paul II used to teach, has started training Polish seminarians for the USSR. Father von Stratten's Aid to the Church in Need, with the help of Mother Angelica, is beaming the Christian message by radio into every corner of the Soviet Union and sending in tons of literature. Some of HLI's anti-abortion films are already being shown to audiences in Ukraine, thanks to our friends.

Some participants from the USSR thought Mikhail Gorbachev wouldn't make it. Most don't trust him, saying he may be a Trojan horse. In his book *Perestroika,* Gorby heaps praise on the priest-murderer Lenin, who invented the death camps later copied by the Nazis.

Volkswagen of Stuttgart, Germany, is building a factory in the USSR to produce cheap cars. But this company has found it almost impossible to organize the workers. After eighty years of persecution, degradation, and subjugation, which snuffed out creativity and any sense of personal responsibility, the Soviet worker has become a kind of robot. He was never allowed to think. He has no work ethic, no dependability, no inclination to follow detailed directions. The sudden, growing freedom befuddles and confuses him. The Soviet proletariat must first be psychologically rehabilitated before it can become part of modern industry. I'll have an in-depth report for you after my visit to the USSR next May—Mary's month.

ABORTION IN THE GERMANYS

In 1974, with comparatively little opposition from the Lutheran and Catholic Churches, the Socialists in the West German parliament passed an abortion-on-demand law covering the first three months of pregnancy. In 1975, the West German Supreme Court declared the law

---

The West German Supreme Court then proceeded to outline "indications" under which babies might indeed be killed.

---

unconstitutional, stating that everyone knows life begins with conception and that, of all peoples on earth, none should understand the value of life better than the Germans, given their bloody history.

The Court then proceeded to outline "indications" under which babies might indeed be killed: for socio-economic reasons and for rape and incest in the first three months of pregnancy; for fetal defects, through the twenty-second week; for the life of the mother and various health reasons, both physical and mental, throughout the pregnancy, "before labor pains"! This outline led to abortion-on-demand, even though the mother had to find a doctor to verify the "indication" and had to be "counseled" beforehand in a nondirective way. I recall sitting in parliament for two whole days listening to the typical pro-abortion lies.

Earlier, in March 1972, the East German Reds legalized abortion-on-demand in the first three months, and for a "defective" child as late as twenty-four weeks. Of course, as always, these limits weren't observed. The Red regime paid for the baby killings, as did West Germany. For sixteen million people, East Germany last year reported

90,000 abortions, but of course there were more than that.

The usual consequences ensued. The birthrate fell so low that East Germany set up the highest family allowances (bribes) in the Western world to induce couples to have children. The birthrate in West Germany is the lowest on earth—1.3 children per "completed" family—and it's only slightly higher in the East.

With the unification of the two Germanys, the question of which abortion law to follow became the most serious bone of contention. The Christian Democratics, the ruling party of West German Chancellor Helmut Kohl, wanted the Western law to prevail. The Bavarian Christian Social Union more or less agreed. The liberal coalition partner, the Free Democratic Party (FDP), the Socialist Democratic Party (SDP), and the Green/Environmental Party ferociously insisted on East Germany's law of abortion-on-demand.

Cardinal Joachim Meisner of Cologne said that he'd rather keep the two Germanys separate than accept the East German law. The presidents of the Catholic and Evangelical Churches, Bishops Karl Lehmann and Martin Kruse, spoke out vigorously against the Eastern law and called a proposed compromise of letting the two zones have separate laws "problematic."

After much wrangling, the politicians decided each Germany would keep its own law for two years. Then a law would be written for the whole country. This two-law arrangement, which is contrary to the German constitution, will produce much "abortion tourism," as they call it in Europe. Abortion-on-demand prevails in both zones, but Western women will go east to avoid the hassles of "counseling" and of getting a doctor to verify "the indication."

In West Germany, abortion remains in the criminal code. In fact, last winter a Bavarian doctor was jailed for not following the minimal requirements. This action brought howls from the feminists, who want abortion to be considered merely a medical procedure. What the law will say two years from now, no one will predict. Some fear the European Parliament will soon demand that all coun-tries in Europe enact uniform abortion laws, or, at least, laws permitting only minor local variations.

Ireland and Malta, the only countries in Europe still forbidding abortion, have already made it clear that they'd leave the European union if it insisted on baby-killing. This departure would mean horrendous economic consequences for these two small countries.

In an effort to defend babies, officials of the World Federation of Doctors, Aktion Leben (the largest right-to-life organization in Germany), and HLI met some months ago to plan an anti-abortion conference, which then took place in Dresden in September. I'll bring you more on this meeting and on the Church in Germany in my next Report.

KNIGHT OF COLUMBUS EXPOSED AS KLAN MEMBER

The 5 October 1990 *New York Post* revealed that the New York state Ku Klux Klan leader William Hoff of Astoria was "an activist in the Catholic Church-backed Knights of Columbus despite the fact that...the Klan has long espoused 'anti-Papist' and anti-Catholic positions." The defiant Hoff proudly says, "I'm a racist," one minute and, "I'm a Catholic," the next, according to the Post.

K of C Supreme Chaplain Bishop Thomas Daily of Brooklyn promptly said there's no way Hoff could consider himself a good Catholic. "Membership in the KKK is incompatible with the teachings of the Catholic Church," he explained. Albert Castello, state deputy of the Knights, told the Post that Hoff could be expelled for "bringing slander [sic] to the Order." Hoff then resigned from the Knights.

If the Knights can drive out Hoff, why can't they drive out the eleven prominent politicians whose votes are killing millions more blacks through abortion than were ever killed through lynchings?

Supreme Knight Dechant and other top Knights assert that they can't act until the bishops declare that the Knights of Death aren't good Catholics. Perhaps they should consult *Faith and Fraternalism,* the history of the order (Harper & Row, 1982). It quotes the apostolic delegate, Archbishop Amleto Cicognani, as saying in 1955,

"The Knights of Columbus is not an organization of the Church. It is a body of Catholic men having an independent status and its own program and its own objectives. It has a right to conduct its business as it sees fit without interference from the hierarchy or the clergy" (p. 395).

A real knight is a soldier who defends the weak no matter what the cost or the danger. When will the Knights' leaders stop hiding behind timid bishops and expel both bigots and baby-killers?

ERRATUM AND APOLOGY

In *Report No. 73* I revealed that in 1974 the New York Knights of Columbus expelled a pro-abort state legislator, thus giving the lie to current Supreme Knight Virgil C. Dechant's assertion that the order lacks the power to kick out politicians such as Gov. Mario Cuomo, Sen. Ted Kennedy, and so on.

Because of an editor's error, we omitted the name of the pro-abort, Anthony Stella, and substituted the name of Martin O'Grady, who in fact had gathered the evidence against Stella. We sincerely apologize to Martin, one of the all-time great prolifers of New York.

THE WORLD'S MOST APOSTOLIC DOCTOR

Yugoslav Dr. Antun Lisec is the most dedicated young European doctor fighting abortion that I know of. A surgeon of no small ability, he is deeply in love with "Holy Mary." Unmarried, he spend as much time as possible showing prolife films, holding conferences for young people, counseling women against abortion, talking to reporters, and so forth.

Antun asked me whether I knew anyone in the USA who'd give him $750 a month for living expenses. He'd leave his medical practice and work full time for the babies, the family, and the Church. Imagine the babies he'd save, the young people he'd persuade to be chaste, the doctors and nurses whose minds he'd change about contraceptive/abortifacient Pills and IUDs, the abortionists he'd convert, and so on, if only his talents could be unleashed!

THANKSGIVING

I'm very tired from my travels and my office workload. But Thanksgiving is just around the corner, and I give thanks to God for sending so many beautiful souls to support, encourage, and pray for me.

This Thanksgiving, my prayer is that the Father of Life will grant you health, happiness, and holiness, and that He'll carefully safeguard any of your loved ones who are in the Mideast war zone.

Children are the only future the Church has (Nigeria, 1988).

The Archbishop of Kaduna, Nigeria, welcomes Fr. Marx.

Hope Amidst the Horrors

No. 75   December 1990

I n my last *Report,* I explained how, after much quarreling, the two Germanys merged. They agreed that each would keep its own abortion law for two years; then they would draft a law for the whole nation.

Western Germany has government-paid baby-killing on demand, despite some meaningless restrictions. The Catholic Church is directly involved: it provides the non-directive "counseling" that the law requires abortion-bound mothers to get. In Eastern Germany, the taxpayers provide abortion-on-demand in the first three months of pregnancy.

According to the best evidence, the sixty million Westerners kill 500,000 unborn babies annually; the sixteen million Easterners kill perhaps 200,000. This means one baby killed for every baby born alive, in a nation with the lowest birthrate in the world—1.3 children per completed family.

The great German prolife authority, Dr. Siegfried Ernst, estimates that the average all-German couple has 1.1 child in a married lifetime; the rest of the birthrate is contributed by the six to eight million foreigners, including almost two million Moslems. The Communist East attained a slightly higher birthrate because the Reds paid the highest family allowances in the world to induce couples to have children.

1,000 MEET TO RESCUE THE FUTURE

In view of the coming debate on the new law and because the Eastern German media report abortion news more honestly than the Western, "Aktion Leben" (Germany's national prolife organization), the World Federation of Doctors Who Respect Human Life, and HLI held a conference on the right to life, and the future of Europe in Dresden (September 20-23) to discuss the whole abortion question. The Catholic bishops financed the meeting, in part. More than 1,000 people from ten countries attended, including many doctors and a surprising number of people from East Germany. HLI's abundant free literature, provided by our benefactors, disappeared in hours.

Before World War II, Dresden was one of Germany's most beautiful and cultured cities. On the night of 13 February 1945, the British Royal Air Force, in revenge for the German destruction of Coventry several years before, destroyed virtually all of Dresden with carefully patterned firebombs.

The residents received only three minutes' warning. More than 100,000 died in the firestorm, as many as perished at Hiroshima or Nagasaki. Forty nuns suffocated in the basement of their convent while praying the rosary. The incendiary bombs set people on fire; even jumping into the Elbe River failed to douse the flames. Ruins of some of Dresden's beautiful buildings are still evident in this once-lovely city that has grown back to 500,000 inhabitants.

To summarize the conference's many fine talks is impossible. Catholic Bishop Joachim Reinelt of Dresden-Meissen hit the mark in a sermon, saying, "Abortion frees not women but men, who then often make female bodies their erotic playthings." Many attendees were surprised to hear some speakers condemn the contraceptive mentality as the gateway to abortion.

The Swiss gynecologist Rudolf Ehmann delivered perhaps the most impressive talk. He reviewed all of the medical literature, proving that the IUD and "die AntiBabyPille" are truly abortifacients. He marshalled massive scientific proof of the lies told to hide the health hazards of the Pill, the IUD, and all artificial/chemical/mechanical birth "control." We'll publish this research as a pamphlet soon; so many bishops, priests, doctors, intellectuals, and lay people seem not to know that in the USA there are far more Pill and IUD abortions than surgical abortions.

Incidentally, Dr. Ehmann received the inspiration for this paper at our World Conference in Irvine, California, in 1988; he's been working on this project, along with others, ever since. Our gatherings inspire hundreds of prolife actions such as these.

The much-jailed Russian dissident psychiatrist Anatolij Korjagin showed how the Marxists used the medical profession as a brutal instrument of ideology. Countess Johanna von Westfalen, member of the West German parliament, traced the deadly evolution of Marx's "To everyone according to his need" to the pro-aborts' "My body is my own." In my hour-long talk, I shared my 82-country experience in fighting the death peddlers over the last twenty-five years.

Max Türkauf, the great Swiss authority on physical chemistry who worked on the A-bomb in France, gave a brilliant talk insisting that, and showing how, New Age religion is far more dangerous than Marxism, on which he's also an authority. It was startling to hear this noted scientist eloquently pleading for prayer and penance in reparation for sin. Privately, he told me he believes only a small flock will remain truly Catholic in Europe, thanks to the prevailing hedonistic materialism, the disloyalty of the theologians, the New Age movement, and the pitiful weakness of the bishops as a whole.

Türkauf also said girls have been serving at Mass in most Swiss parishes. When the girls started, the altar boys quit; now many of the altar girls, bored with serving, have also quit, and so priests often have altar nobodies. Türkauf and others insisted that the Catholic Church in Switzerland is in far worse shape than that in West Germany and Austria—even worse than in Holland, where at least they have one orthodox national seminary (at Rolduc).

HORROR STORIES FROM THE GERMAN CHURCH

Of the twelve national hierarchies that dissented to *Humanae Vitae* in 1968, none did it with more sophistication, perhaps, than the scholarly Germans, goaded on by such wild theologians as the late Father Karl Rahner, SJ.

They reaffirmed their vigorous dissent in 1975 at a national synod in Würtzburg. There, the theologians again shouted down the few bishops who had begun to see the truth, such as the perceptive Bishop Rudolf Graber of Regensburg, now retired.

Today, fewer than 20 percent of German Catholics

attend Sunday Mass. Many young couples "live together," divorce is increasing, and the low birthrate has made

---

The situation in some German seminaries defies belief, especially in Bonn and Aachen.

---

wealthy Germany the fastest-dying nation on earth.

Conditions in many Western seminaries often are atrocious, but the situation in some German seminaries defies belief, especially in Bonn and Aachen. Masturbation is made light of, the Mother of God is ignored or ridiculed as a "Flittchen" (a silly, cheap, mindless girl), daily Mass is abandoned and the rosary is derided.

No wonder many German priests offer Mass as seldom as possible, no longer say the Divine Office, and rarely, if ever, pray the rosary. A highly perceptive, dedicated German Dominican nun told me, "Many priests, especially the young, have too much money. They live in great comfort. They've become social workers at best and functionaries at worst."

Seminary professors question whether God revealed Himself in Jesus. They debate how and why the Canon of the Mass should be changed, and whether a celibate life is possible. A spiritual director once told his seminarians, "I beg you, fully think through, just for once, that for our time prime movers such as Marx, Gandhi, and the pioneers of feminism, concerned about freeing and saving human beings, may actually be tools in God's hands."

Letting young women into seminary housing isn't unknown. The condoms found in one seminary would suggest that the rosary wasn't the future priests' favorite pastime. Some seminary rooms are decorated with pornography; obscene videos and TV shows are watched freely. And there's evidence that some professors have liaisons with women. Professors and rectors say they know nothing about these scandals.

Seminarians are allowed to date girls. No wonder young priests in the diocese of Aachen gathered signatures asking for an end to celibacy! During "celibate weekends" when they're supposed to be studying celibacy, seminarians vehemently proclaim their right to eroticism ("Zartlichkeit"). One seminary director admits he urged seminarians to "sleep" with girls. Women are often said to have keys to seminarians' rooms. Those seminarians who want to live a chaste life are ridiculed.

Few go to confession, because sin is no longer learned as sin. Homosexuality isn't unknown; even the wrongness of homosexual acts is debated. Penance services take place, rarely with an opportunity to confess personally. Some seminarians never confess sacramentally. In one seminary, after Mass begins there's an hour-long (!) pause for confession or meditation—contrary to Church rubrics.

Vatican II's suggestion that every priest offer Mass daily is widely ignored. Noncelebrating priests often sit in the congregation. In some housing where seminarians have rooms, two-thirds of the roomers are secular students, including women. Other seminarians live in the city.

Teachings about the Eucharist question the Real Presence. One professor said praying to the "bread" of the Eucharist was psychologically difficult. Therefore, "one might as well put a good-for-nothing alcoholic in the tabernacle as the Holy Bread," he asserted.

Seminarians are taught that they must learn to offer a creative liturgy under various forms. Abuses are many. Communion on the tongue is a forgotten custom, of course. Mass is offered at an ordinary table, "a sit-down table Mass." The Mass is always a "feast," a "meal," "a celebration"—little or nothing is said about a sacrifice. Sometimes the songs border on the blasphemous.

Woe to those seminarians who dissent from the dissenters and wish to be faithful to the Church! Where possible, they're kept from attending an orthodox seminary program during what's called "the free semester." Pope John Paul II, Archbishop Johannes Dyba of Fulda, and Cardinal Joseph Ratzinger are derided and mocked. Nowhere is the Vicar of Christ hated more than in Germany—except, perhaps, in Switzerland or Holland.

Some seminarians lose their faith. A few have committed suicide. Others escape to saner seminaries, even to other countries. Still others join Archbishop LeFebvre or the St. Peter's Society Seminary at Wigratzbad, where, after only two years, there are some 120 major seminarians. No wonder Europe has become a mission field where more than 3,000 American fundamentalist missionaries keep busy.

PLANNED PARENTHOOD & THEOLOGIANS AT WORK

Much of the blame for the moral collapse in Germany can be laid squarely at the door of Planned Parenthood (PP), known in West Germany as "Pro Familia" and in East Germany as "Ehe und Familie" (Marriage and the Family). Pro Familia appeared in Germany in 1952, the very year the International Planned Parenthood Federation (IPPF)

> *Much of the blame for the moral collapse in Germany can be laid squarely at the door of Planned Parenthood.*

---

began operation in London. In fact, IPPF's first president was a German, Hans Harmsen. Ehe und Familie has built up 200 contraception/abortion centers over many years. Someday someone will have to expose the sordid collaboration between PP and the murderous Communists.

Helping to destroy the German Church were many pseudo-sophisticated theologians whose theoretical, often erring theologizing makes our Fathers Curran, McBrien, McCormick, and so on, seem shallow by comparison. For example, right now good Bishop Karl Braun of Eichstatt is trying to minimize the enormous harm done by the many books and mass-media appearances of the Modernist, syncretistic, Freudian psychotherapist priest, Eugene Drewermann. In "the spirit of Vatican II," Father Drewermann cleverly attacks virtually all of the dogmatic and moral teaching of the Church.

Last January, 163 theologians from the German-speaking countries and Holland condemned the pope in their "Cologne Declaration." Other theologians soon joined them; now the Catholic Theological Society of America has drafted a similar attack. The Cologne Declaration accused His Holiness of abusing his authority, of failing to exercise adequate consultation in the appointment of bishops, and of irresponsibly upholding that hated sign of contradiction, *Humanae Vitae.*

The prolife Lutheran intellectual, Dr. Ernst, has eloquently refuted the theologians' dissent to *Humanae Vitae*. Next month we'll publish his brilliant counterthrust in a pamphlet. It was Siegfried Ernst, by the way, who told the late dissenting Cardinal Julius Döpfner of Munich that a cardinal shouldn't need a Lutheran doctor to tell him to obey Pope Paul VI's encyclical! As the German Church declined, Cardinal Döpfner saw, too late, that the pope was right.

In the 1970s, Germany legalized divorce, pornography, prostitution, sterilization, and baby-killing. Today the country is talking about legalizing euthanasia. Last April 25, the minister of justice introduced a bill allowing the forced sterilization of incompetent adults when their guardians consent. The rationale? "The right to pleasurable sexual intercourse without the fear of an unwanted, irresponsible pregnancy."

Behind this agitation, of course, is Pro Familia, which propagates the dangerous lie that everyone, married or single, at any age, has a right to sexual intercourse and that sex must be made available in every possible way for handicapped people and residents of senior citizens' homes. By the way, the most sophisticated and offensive sex-"education" materials and pornography I've seen in eighty-two countries are produced in Germany, the world's chief pornographer.

In Germany, confessions are rare, vocations are few, and the abundant theology students include many women. The feminist, Socialist, New Age, and environmentalist movements are powerful. Natural family planning (NFP) is just emerging.

Cologne's late Cardinal Josef Höffner once said that when it comes to NFP, Germany is a Third World country. Shortly before his death, as president of the German bishops he urged total adherence to *HV*—to no avail.

(Strangely, when the harmful dissident theologian, Father Franz Böckle, retired, Cardinal Höffner praised him to the skies!)

Hoping to get things going some years ago, Japan's NFP authority, Father Anthony Zimmerman, and I discussed NFP for hours with Monsignor Vincent Platz, a high-ranking advisor for marital affairs in the Church bureaucracy. Monsignor Platz's arrogant resistance was exceeded only by his abysmal ignorance of NFP.

Germans are famous for their *Sachlichkeit* (factuality or realism) and *Gründlichkeit* (thoroughness). So it's astonishing to find included in their school books Darwin's and Haeckel's theories of human evolution, i.e., the discredited idea that the preborn baby goes through various animal stages before he becomes human. This inclusion is especially true of East German texts. In this kind of environment, the prolife movement is weak, but the country does have great defenders of preborn children such as Dr. Ernst, Dr. Georg Götz, Dr. Alfred Häussler, Walter Ramm, Roland Rösler, and the persecuted Father Otto Maier, the only active prolife priest.

SHEPHERDS BETRAY THEIR SHEEP

Seemingly oblivious to West Germany's virtual abortion-on-demand, and incredibly overlooking the Church's direct involvement in abortion via pre-abortion "counseling," the liberal Bishop Karl Lehmann, president of the German hierarchy, has all but abandoned Germany's innocents—with typical involved, heavy, Germanic reasoning (or

---

This unbelievable abandonment of most of Germany's unborn babies is the German Church's official position.

---

rationalizing). In so many words, he's saying the present law need not be changed essentially, except for the socio-economic indications.

This unbelievable abandonment of most of Germany's unborn babies is the German Church's official position, even if a few bishops don't accept it. Bishop Lehmann and his cohorts have handed over their shepherding role to "progressive" bureaucrats in the bishops' conference, such as Dr. Karl Panzer, Monsignor Platz, and the moral theologians, who mostly teach situation ethics. It's a frightening state of affairs. Bishop Lehmann recently said the Church's biggest problem is the question of women priests, whom he favors.

Bishop Reinelt Lettman of Münster has appeared in print against *HV*. On TV, Hildesheim's Bishop Josef Homeyer once defended priestesses and damned *HV*. In a pastoral on marriage, Bishop Homeyer, like Bishop Ludwig Averkamp of Osnabrück, absolutized "conscience" over *HV*, more or less approved divorce (and Communion for the divorced as a matter of conscience), and wrote that couples who love each other and are committed to a future marriage may, understandably, have sexual intercourse.

Bishop Lehmann, a defender of Hans Küng and a man over-impressed by liberation theology, has said virtually the same things. When the abortifacient character of the Pill and IUD was pointed out to Bishop Homeyer, he, like other German bishops, said nothing. Meanwhile, Bishop Ernst Gutting of Speyer enthuses about women priests.

One bishop (name withheld) likes to point out the supposed benefits of contraception, saying sixty million Germans kill fewer babies than do thirty-eight million Poles. The truth is, the Pill-happy Germans abort many more children, because of the early abortions induced by the many women on the Pill.

Three years ago Archbishop Dyba asked all 400 of his pastors to ring their church bells for fifteen minutes at noon on Holy Innocents' Day (December 28) in mourning for the half million German babies killed every year by abortionists. Last year, at their annual meeting in Fulda, the German bishops agreed to do so in every diocese. When the story hit the press there was a huge uproar. The bishops were called anti-women, unfeeling, discriminatory, inhuman, uncivil, disloyal, and so forth.

Many bishops then proved to be what many good Germans accuse them of being: cowards. Bells rang in some dioceses but were silenced in others. In still others, the bishops left it up to the pastors. In short, there was no uniform, eloquent Catholic protest against the legalized mass murder of babies. In this public-relations disaster, the feminists and the abortionists won again. Now the bishops have decided on a bland annual "Week for Life" in June, with meetings, speeches, pilgrimages, and Masses. This tokenism will cause them no embarrassment.

GET YOUR CATHOLIC CONDOMS

Every second year since 1948, the Church has sponsored Katholikentag (Catholic Day), a national gathering to discuss problems in the Church, family, society, and politics. This year the meeting was held in Berlin; an unbelievable 130,000 people came. The powerful lay bureaucracy of the bishops' conference more or less decides the program for this affair, with input from Modernist theologians and their sycophants; so some strange theologizing went on.

The dissident Father Böckle explained away the moral difference between the Pill and NFP. The infallible Father Böckle pontificated that forbidding contraception was the tragedy of Pope John Paul II. Astonishingly, he said love justifies any sexual activity ("Es gibt keine hinreichende Begründung für Sündhaftiget der Liebe"). (About two years ago, Father Böckle called Father Carlo Caffara, OP, the pope's theologian on marriage, "stupid and satanic" for defending *HV*. On another occasion, when the abortifacient character of the Pill was pointed out to him, he said that was no reason to stay off the Pill!)

German Catholic charities mounted an exhibit. Part of it showed two teenagers fornicating, with the caption, "And so they have always done it. Today they do it with a condom." Condoms were given out freely at the exhibit; bishops, priests, and nuns passed by, but no one protested.

Also present were members of "Die Initiative Kirche von unten" ("Church from Below"), consisting of angry ex-priests, frenzied feminists, Catholic-haters, disgruntled intellectuals, and other ultra-liberals. Bureaucrats ejected Walter Ramm's right-to-lifers. One reason for their exclusion is that the healthy part of the German prolife movement reminds the nation that contraception is the gateway to abortion. This understanding, of course, is anathema to the Pill-swallowers, the feminists, and their justifying theologians.

But there were some sane voices, too. Cardinal Joachim Meisner, Archbishop of Cologne, Europe's largest diocese (928 parishes), said he'd rather have no German reunification if it meant adopting the East German law. What he overlooked, though, is that the Western law is actually worse than the Eastern.

He also forgot that on 26 November 1973, a year before the final abortion law was passed, the German bishops (with Cardinal Döpfner as president) and the Evangelical Council of Lutheran Bishops issued a joint document allowing abortion if the abortionist said there was serious danger to the mother's life and the possibility of serious, lasting damage to her health. The German bishops failed to foresee what legalized abortion would be and, except for a few, are failing to oppose baby-killing properly even now. (One breath of fresh air in the German Church is the orthodox journal *Theologisches,* edited by Father Johannes Bökmann. Along with two other German publications, it published HLI's 42-point article "What Bishops Could Do about Abortion.")

One of the German Church's worst horror stories is its collaboration with the abortion industry by providing government-required nondirective "counseling." The

> *One of the German Church's worst horror stories is its collaboration with the abortion industry by providing government-required nondirective "counseling."*

government funds both Pro Familia "counseling" centers and those of the churches. But most girls are served by the infamous Pro Familia.

The president of the German Catholic Women's Society, Dr. Elisabeth Buschmann, and other prominent Catholic women—e.g., "Catholic" former Health Minister Rita Süssmuth, now president of the parliament—have stressed that no pressure may be put upon abortion-bound women: their "consciences" must remain free. By now an estimated 50 percent of all German wives have aborted one or more babies.

Most German bishops, of course, insist they're not collaborating. At most, they say, it's remote, material cooperation, justified because some babies are saved (in fact, few are). Among prolifers and Catholic intellectuals there's a continuous, angry, agonizing discussion over this situation. Mysteriously, informed Vatican officials have taken no action.

How will the hierarchy extricate itself from this shameful entanglement? Sensitive to the need to save face, the liberal Bishop Walter Casper of Stuttgart is working on it. Those most responsible for the tragic situation are Father Böckle, the moral theologian Father Johannes Gründel, and key advisors to the bishops.

Germany is enormously rich, the world's number-two exporter, so efficient that Germans enjoy the shortest workday of any industrialized people. They're very generous to the poor overseas, through money given to the bishops from Church taxes (some 30 million D-Mark yearly—about $20 million). It almost seems as if German Catholics excuse their non-churchgoing and non-practice by their charitable giving. Speaking in Germany, Pope John Paul II gently but pointedly reminded them that their indirect generosity was no substitute for religious observance.

Meanwhile, the fast-growing Moslems, who have built mosques all over Germany, recently shocked the nation when they proposed building Europe's largest mosque in the historic Catholic city of Aachen (the city of Charlemagne), costing an estimated 60 million D-Mark. It would include a university, a congress hall, a sports palace, a library, a cultural center, training schools, and other facilities. The Socialists favor it; the liberals and the ecumaniacs, including wild theologians, say one must be "religiously tolerant." Many Christians are appalled. Where does the money come from? It's a tightly kept secret.

EAST GERMAN PROLIFERS EMERGE

I should tell you something about the sixteen million East Germans under the Reds. Eastern Germany is mostly Protestant, with Catholics making up 6 percent of the population. Catholics have six dioceses covering the five states. Their priests told me that only about 80,000 Catholics out of 1.4 million practice their faith. The Reds allowed two Catholic seminaries (at Erfurt and Berlin) but forbade women to study theology. Under the Marxists, religious education came to a standstill; now West Germany's worst religious ed is moving in.

I was astonished by the amount of pornography already flooding Dresden and by the filthy movies shown everywhere. While driving the 180 kilometers from Berlin to Dresden, we hardly saw one person; the region is almost empty. East Germany was the best off among the Soviet satellites, but the ravages of Communism are glaring, including the poor roads, the destroyed forests, the polluted environment, and the run-down buildings.

The extent of pollution in Eastern Europe was supposedly classified information, Communism's dirtiest secret. Belching smokestacks disfigure the landscape; unsafe nuclear reactors are decaying. The West German government is shutting down five dangerous East German nuclear plants. Forests are dying, many lakes and streams are fishless, and blackened cities are decorated with pollution-eroded statues.

In the East German industrial center of Leipzig, life expectancy is six years less than the national average. Four of every five children develop chronic bronchitis or heart ailments by age seven. In the industrial heartland, at any given time, some 60 percent of the people suffer from respiratory disease because of the choking fumes from burning brown coal. Almost 9 percent of the farmland has been ruined by pollution and overdoses of fertilizers. Some estimate that 80 percent of the forests may already be damaged by acid rain. One-tenth of the population must drink water that doesn't meet public health standards. In other former satellites, conditions are even worse.

The dreaded secret police, the *Stasi*, employed 85,000 full-time agents and some 500,000 part-time informants. Their names and files haven't been made public. There's a great deal of suspicion and anxiety; reportedly, the Reds even bugged confessionals. The former leaders of the Stasi now work for the Soviet KGB, which reaches into the

USSR's armed forces, the West German government, and many other German institutions.

Now land and property stolen by the Reds are to be given back—but to whom, when there are multiple claims? The former Red bosses and the *Stasi* grabbed much property and left a huge mess for the West Germans to clean up, to cost an estimated $750 billion. In the eastern region, the GNP dropped 10 percent this year; 1.4 million workers are unemployed.

East Germany supports only a fledgling right-to-life movement called KALEB, which stands for "Kooperative Arbeit Leben ehrfurchtig bewahren," meaning "A Cooperative Labor to Honorably Protect Life." This ecumenical effort is mostly of Evangelical inspiration, having begun officially last January 27 in Leipzig after the East shed Communism.

I spoke to members at a seminar last year in Senden, West Germany, where they had come for some updating. The foundress, nurse, and mother-of-six Gisela Kohler said only one Catholic priest supported her at first. Her group collected 42,000 signatures against abortion. The unusual thing about KALEB is its awareness of the role of contraception in the antilife movement. Pray for them!

SHAW DEFENDS KNIGHTS OF DEATH

K of C spokesman Russell Shaw continues to defend "the right arm of the Church" for harboring notorious pro-abortion politicians. Says he in *The Wanderer* (25 October 1990), "We'll let our leaders (the bishops) lead; we will not be led by the nose by Father Paul Marx." Alas, in the sixteenth century, Shaw and Supreme Knight Virgil Dechant probably would have blindly followed the sixteen English bishops out of the Church when the prelates swore allegiance to King Henry VIII rather than the pope. I commend to both the example of St. Thomas More.

Pro-Life President Kenneth Kaunda of Zambia greets Fr. Marx in Lusaka, the capital.

Fr. Marx with his prolife friend Christi Hockel of Walnut Creek, California.

A warm welcome by the gracious Filipinos and Filipinas in 1975.

Fr. Marx is on the phone endlessly—often with prolifers overseas.

In the bustling warehouse at HLI World Headquarters in Maryland, Fr. Marx, Cara Polcha, Wojciech Pawlowski and Dave Malat ship materials all over the world every day.

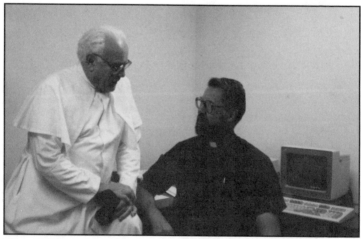

The OSBs—Fr. Marx and his Special Assistant, Fr. Habiger

His Eminence Jaime Cardinal Sin and Fr. Marx in Manila in 1975.

The tireless Magaly Llaguno of HLI Miami, telling it like it is.

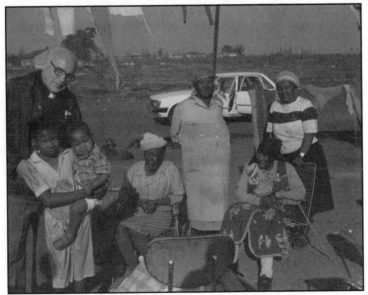

All children are wanted children: Fr. Marx with South Africans in Soweto.

Now you'll understand why Fr. Marx has had two hernia operations!

On one of Fr. Marx's earlier journeys, he made three friends in Taipei, Taiwan.

Fr. Marx confers with clergy worldwide about threats to the family—here with the bishop of Spiecez, Czechoslovakia.

Latin America Chooses Death

No. 76   January 1991

I n 1972 I celebrated my twenty-fifth anniversary as a priest by visiting virtually every country in Latin America over a three-month period. My goal was to get something started against the pro-abortionists in the only Catholic continent on earth. After nearly dying from altitude sickness in La Paz, Bolivia, the highest city in the world, I returned home certain that Latin America would become a continent of death.

COLOMBIA: PLANNED BARRENHOOD'S MODEL COUNTRY

Now, eighteen years later, after spending eight days in the Colombian cities of Barranquilla and Bogatá in October, I'm even more certain that the population imperialists will succeed; they've brought abortion-on-demand to the beautiful people of this fascinating country.

Thanks to baby-killing, family-destroying Planned Parenthood (PP), abortion is already common, although illegal, in every country of Latin America (dying Uruguay is the only nation that has relaxed its law). The groundwork for abortion was laid in Colombia in 1965 when ProFamilia (as PP calls itself, although ContraFamilia would be more accurate) moved in with its usual bags of money and its selfproclaimed expertise.

Colombian law forbids abortion except to save the life of the mother; it punishes abortionist and mother equally with one-to-three-year prison sentences. If her pregnancy resulted from a proven rape, the woman would have to serve only four months.

In 1975 the government made its first attempt to strip unborn children of protection. Colombia might have legal abortion today had it not been for two events that seem providential, at least to the Colombians. One involved Emilio Urrea, the loudest pro-abort politician, who was running for the senate this year. On Good Friday, while playing polo, the Kennedy-style "Catholic" Urrea fell off his horse; he died instantly. He'd claimed that 40,000

Colombian women died annually from illegal abortions (in another context, PP says 37,000 women die from illegal abortions in *all* of Latin America).

The other act of God befell Anna Sixta, formerly Colombia's feminist representative for women's affairs at the UN. She had lost her position because of a change of government and was to take Urrea's place. She died in a plane crash.

In no country of the world, perhaps, is PP more firmly rooted and less opposed than in Colombia, where the government is a silent, cooperating partner. ProFamilia's deceptive official title is "Asociación Pro-Bienestar de la Familia Colombiana," i.e., "Association for the Betterment of the Colombian Family."

Its members boast that they've "become one of the major family-planning associations in the world" (see PP's "Country Factsheets"). In 1988 the UN Fund for Population Activities (UNFPA) gave this infamous organization its annual depopulation award. The Colombian government recently presented its highest civilian honor, the Cruz de Boyaca, to Dr. Fernando Tamayo, the founder of ProFamilia. A ceremony at the presidential palace paid tribute to his twenty-five years of depopulation efforts.

P.P.'S WAR ON FERTILITY

From 1966 to 1986 there was a frightening drop in Colombia's birthrate, from 44 to 29 per 1,000 people, and

---

In every town and in every poor neighborhood, Planned Parenthood operates "health stands," which are nothing but camouflaged birth-prevention centers.

---

therefore a slowdown in population growth. Contraceptive/abortifacient use is high; more than 65 percent of couples "at risk" use them.

In every town and in every poor neighborhood PP operates "health stands," which are nothing but camouflaged birth-prevention centers. In the countryside, its workers supply mobile units. PP runs massive, intensive sterilization campaigns in both city and countryside.

"One day," writes Ariel Pinilla Serrano, president of the Corporación Universal Pro Vita, a small prolife group in Barranquilla, "when I arrived in a town to explain the consequences of contraception, a woman told me in exactly these words, 'Doctor, you are late; we have all been castrated; there are only two left and the promoters of the health stands are persecuting them. This is very painful.'"

ProFamilia's sterility squads finance their dirty work with your tax money. They travel from house to house pushing sterilization; even women who are only twenty-five and have only one child are often sterilized. About 1984, poor country women, mostly Indians, were trucked into town, tricked into being sterilized, kept for a few hours, and then abandoned to the streets. A bishop's protest put a stop to this practice.

The minister of education is aiming sex "education" at children in public elementary schools. Materials produced by the National Education Department assert that virginity has no value, that masturbation is normal, and that contraception is a modern necessity. Of course, all of this propaganda serves the purposes of PP by creating conditions that favor the distribution of contraceptives and, at the same time, undermine the traditional family values that always stand in PP's way.

The government actually takes part in this attack upon the poor and their children, giving them a nutritional supplement made of soy and wheat called "Bienestarina." Allegedly, it contains an anti-fertility substance. A doctor said he heard this allegation from an employee of the manufacturer. Unfortunately, prolifers have been unable to get a lab to analyze the product, which they want to denounce publicly.

Young women are sometimes administered the injectible abortifacient Depo-Provera for their menstrual problems; as a result, a doctor claimed, university students sometimes had no menstrual period for two years. (Depo-Provera is so dangerous it's forbidden in the USA.) Several doctors told me they'd treated women who'd been sterilized without their knowing it, after giving birth.

TEN THOUSAND DEATH STATIONS

ProFamilia runs forty-eight major "clinics," three of them exclusively for men. But because of *machismo,* Latin American men shy away from sterilization, the barnyard approach to birth control. ProFamilia knows best, though, and started a pilot vasectomy center and program in Barranquilla, Colombia's fourth-largest city. Throughout the country, ProFamilia maintains almost 10,000 community supply points that distribute contraceptives/abortifacients; it has also tried various marketing approaches to make these products available at low prices in drugstores, supermarkets and cooperatives.

A young Colombian doctor told me ProFamilia performed at least 100,000 female sterilizations every year. They broadcast by radio where their doctors will be on certain days, invite the women to get "fixed," keep them for two hours, and then dismiss them. In their mobile sterilization units they do only laparoscopy sterilizations. They charge just $4, compared with $600 for childbirth-plus-sterilization in a hospital.

ProFamilia reaches the public through propaganda campaigns on radio and TV, and in newspapers and magazines, especially those that young people read. They're often to be found in the public schools giving raw sex lessons and sometimes get invited by an unwitting priest or nun-principal to speak at a Catholic high school. During these talks, PP agents recommend condoms and sometimes even hand them out, as protection against AIDS (!); of course, they also invite the captive audience to visit their "counseling" centers. Their latest stunt was to set up a "youth clinic" in Bogotá.

ProFamilia plays an important role in training birth-prevention personnel from government on down, as PP does in many Third World countries. ProFamilia has trained more than 2,500 "health" workers, half of whom are foreigners.

Bogotá conducts two large, illegal abortion centers that are well-known. One is run privately by doctors charging high prices, whereas ProFamilia's "Center for Focused Birth" kills babies for less money.

Ask a typical Colombian priest, doctor, or teacher the

number of abortions, and he'll throw up his hands and say, "Many," "Very, very many," or, "God only knows!" Indeed, the number is large, and growing. The resistance is so weak. As elsewhere, so many people just don't know that PP is a coiled snake. Those who do know lack equipment and literature to fight the PP monster.

The most common means of birth prevention are withdrawal, the Pill, the IUD, and the condom. How many couples have been neutered, especially among the poor, is ProFamilia's secret. It's the rarest of priests who speaks out against contraception, abortifacients, or sterilization from the pulpit and the rare priest who even talks about abortion. Lay prolife leaders are disappointed that the bishops, as a rule, say almost nothing about contraception and too little about abortion. The prelates seem all too passive, apparently fearing the government.

BISHOPS DEFEND THEIR LAMBS

In 1984, however, Medellin's fearless, 55-year-old Cardinal Alfonso Lopez Trujillo, who escaped assassination by drug lords three times, spoke out strongly against contraception and abortion. On 29 February 1988 the cardinal wrote a stinging protest to the secretary general of the UN over its depopulation policies. As president of the Colombian National Bishops' Conference, he sent a most encouraging message to our world conference in Miami last April.

Recently the pope appointed him president of the Pontifical Council for the Family, to succeed the ailing Cardinal Edouard Gagnon. We congratulate the cardinal and pledge him our total support. (An emergency prevented my chatting with him during my stay in Colombia.)

Last year Archbishop Dario Castrillon of Pereira attacked abortion strongly, called for a government investigation, and demanded closure of the illegal abortion mills. An estimated one-half of the abortion mills were shut down; abortion advertising in the newspapers has almost ceased. It's often said that Colombia's contracepting upper and middle classes readily abort their babies, whereas the poor have abortion *forced* on them.

There's one thing I've always noticed about Latin

American priests and nuns: they shy away from talking about sexuality and therefore about the important, demanding commandment/virtue of chastity. Nor do many Latin priests enthuse about celibacy.

Promoting chastity is a subject for which, obviously, Latin priests and religious don't get properly prepared in their seminary and religious training. (Do ours?) This lack of attention to chastity, along with a legacy of Spanish sexploitation of the Indians, may explain, in part, why an enormous amount of sexual sin exists in Latin America.

Father Alfonso P. Llano, SJ, the former dean of the Jesuits' Pontificia Universidad Javeriana, writes a widely read Sunday column in Bogotá's largest newspaper, El Tiempo. In it he ever so subtly knocks Pope John Paul II and rejects *Humanae Vitae*, while insisting he thinks much like His Holiness. He has written and said that priests shouldn't talk about bedroom morality because they know nothing about it. It didn't bother this Jesuit that doctors who graduated from Javeriana under his deanship were trained to dispense artificial methods of birth prevention, even the abortifacient Pill and IUD.

As in other countries, most intellectuals provide little help to the fledgling prolife movement. There are five Catholic universities in Bogotá besides Javeriana: San Buenaventura, Gran Colombia, Universidad Catolica, the Christian Brothers' Universidad de La Salle, Santo Tomás, and Opus Dei's new La Sabana. La Sabana, Universidad

> *As in other countries, most intellectuals provide little help to the fledgling prolife movement.*

Catolica, and La Salle are a breath of fresh air in an intellectual environment polluted by "progressive" Jesuits.

Brother Juan Vargas Muñoz, president of La Salle, wants to set up a whole prolife unit in his university library, along with prolife programs. I pledged that our benefactors would generously supply the materials.

Among Colombia's worst problems, of course, is the drug plague. It's everywhere, and it's highly organized. Some keen observers say this scourge will never be eliminated, so entrenched are the wealthy drug lords, who work with the Red guerrillas. The drug lords command an estimated 6,000 hired killers. Surprisingly, drugs aren't a big problem among the youth, just as homosexuality seems rare. Colombians tell you frankly that the drug curse will end only when the voracious U.S. appetite for drugs ends.

A PARADISE THAT NEEDS PEOPLE

Resource-rich Colombia, as large as Texas and New Mexico combined, is South America's fourth-largest country. This enormously rich, underdeveloped land lies at the top end of South America. It has both Atlantic and Pacific coasts, with a connection to Panama jutting up between them.

Colombia is a land of cultural and topographic contrasts, rugged in terrain and divided into five distinct zones by the three-branched Andes Mountains chain. Many islands would make ideal tourist havens if it were not for the drug-related violence; they have a tremendous potential for development, as does everything else in this unique, fascinating country. There are thirty-one "departments" or states.

Colombia knows only one season, unless rainy and windy periods constitute seasons. Because of frequent rain and almost universal sunshine, anything and everything seems to grow. The varying levels of terrain, on which different foods can be raised, enhance the country's potential, as do the long ocean shorelands.

Some 90 percent of the world's emeralds come from Colombia. It's a rare Yanqui who hasn't eaten a Colombian banana or tasted Colombia's famous coffee, which makes up 50 percent of the country's exports. Colombia produces some of its own petroleum needs and owns an almost limitless supply of natural gas, some of which it exports to the USA and other countries.

A somewhat homogeneous population, Colombians emerge from three ethnic types: Spanish, Indian (the dominant group), and black. Briefly, 60 percent of the population is Mestizo (mixed Spanish and Indian) and 14 percent mulatto. Of the remaining 26 percent, 20 percent is Caucasian, 4 percent black, and 2 percent pure Indian.

WILL GUERRILLAS DE-CHRISTIANIZE COLOMBIA?

Colombia gained its independence from Spain in 1819. Despite a long history of democracy, the country has endured its share of political unrest. The present constitution allows only three political parties: Liberal, Conservative, and Communist (now Socialist). Six guerrilla groups of varying sizes exist, mostly in the countryside.

Only two are still fighting. They make forays into the cities, kidnapping daily (for extortion), and pillaging and preying on the citizenry. Three groups are Communist-inspired. Several are talking peace with the government of Liberal César Gaviria Trujillo, inaugurated as president on August 7, after the assassination of several other candidates. The 1,500-member National Liberation Army was founded by a renegade Spanish priest; it specializes in attacking oil, coal, and natural-resource projects.

The Liberal government has been working to secularize the country—to gradually destroy the Church's influence on society. On December 9, left-wing ex-rebels of the M-19 guerrilla movement won the most seats in elections for a national constitutional assembly that will write a new constitution beginning in February.

The feared and violent M-19 laid down its arms last March in exchange for government pardons and permission to form a political party. Their leaders say they've mellowed and moved toward the center. But they'll continue the Liberals' policy of reducing the Church's influence and may even put abortion into the constitution.

Colombia is 95 percent Catholic, with the Pentecostals and other sects moving in fast with much money and literature, and many radio stations. Every one of the forty-five dioceses operates at least one minor seminary; there are many major seminaries, too. Vocations are decidedly up, although a highly perceptive priest told me too many seminarians have "a vocation to the seminary but not to Christ." There's a shortage of priests, and so parishes are often huge.

The country has about 5,000 priests and 12,000 nuns.

The 240 Christian Brothers have eight novices. The Sisters of Charity of St. Vincent de Paul run two provinces, with 1,500 nuns and 37 novices. (They begged us for help.) The Jesuits, Franciscans, and Salesians form the largest religious orders, with U.S. Benedictines allegedly running the two best high schools in Bogotá: San Carlos and Santa Maria.

The annual natural population increase is 2.3 percent and there are seventy people per square mile. The infant mortality rate is exceedingly high, 48 per 1,000 live births. The total fertility rate is 3.4 children per woman, down sharply from preceding generations and still falling.

In 1978 Colombia recorded one of the highest cervical-cancer rates in the world. The chief cause of this cancer is early intercourse with multiple partners. VD, too, is rife in Colombia. AIDS has also struck, with an estimated 150,000 victims in a nation of thirty-two million people. And, as always in foreign countries, good people complain about pervasive, pornographic videos and films arriving from the USA.

The per-capita income in 1986 was $1,112. The minimum wage is $90 per month. The inflation rate is 30 percent; unemployment is 15 percent. Several told me that 2 percent of Colombians live like kings and queens, 18 percent are middle class, and the other 80 percent are very, very poor.

On the plus side, the adult literacy rate in 1982 was 85.2 percent, 91 percent of the population have safe water, and there's one physician for every 2,000 people (*vs.* 1:800 in the USA). In 1983, 68 percent of the population had adequate sanitary facilities. Because of a massive national vaccination program in 1984, Colombia has improved from a rather unhealthy nation to one of the healthiest in the developing world.

SEMINARIANS, MED STUDENTS, HIGH SCHOOLERS EAT UP PROLIFE MESSAGE

Over three days in hot and humid Barranquilla, I gave five lectures, spoke twice in bilingual Catholic high schools, gave two newspaper interviews, did a forty-minute TV program, was the guest on a twenty-five-minute question/ answer show on national radio (with a feminist moderator), and addressed 120 totally interested major seminarians for ninety minutes. (I promised the last group that my friends would buy them a projector and prolife films.)

In a three-hour session at a medical school, future doctors expressed shock at seeing our abortion videos. They gobbled up the abundant prolife literature I'd brought with me. My partner made rosaries available, and you should have seen the scramble for them! This enthusiasm would prevail only in Latin America.

I had a remarkable experience at the coed Marymount

In a three-hour session at a medical school, future doctors expressed shock at seeing our abortion videos.

High School, where girls predominate. It's headed by a magnificent, orthodox U.S. nun, Sister Johanna Gunniffe, from Tarrytown, New York; the faculty is mostly lay. In more than forty years of addressing high school students, I've never before heard so many intelligent questions. I enjoyed a similar experience at the (Catholic) American-British International High School in the same city.

U.S.-educated Dr. Edgardo Llanos, an engineer and the rector of a local university, insists on heading HLI's branch in Barranquilla. With the help of his family, he organized an excellent program for me in that city. Many nuns, some brothers, and several priests asked for audio-visual aids and literature.

Bogotá, higher in the mountains, was delightfully cool. I spent an evening with about twenty-five youth leaders, among them young doctors and lawyers. This session, too, I shall never forget. All were gung-ho to save their country and their Church! They knew their faith and their enemy. I promised them much prolife material from the generosity of supporters and will work with them to the maximum.

I find it hard to comprehend, as some told me, that about 40 percent of Catholics still attend Mass almost every Sunday in the cities. All churches are filled to overflowing on Sundays. I counted six pages of Catholic church listings in the six-million-name Bogotá city telephone book. On weekdays, some churches are filled at each of three Masses. Colombia runs a great many Catholic high schools, financially supported (minimally) by the state. It's perhaps the healthiest Catholic country in Latin America. When he visited here, the pope politely said as much.

The prolife movement is unorganized nationally but supports good little groups here and there. No one has been more effective than "Mrs. Pro-life," Astrid de Bayer, who fifteen years ago began the Fundación Derecho a Nacer (Foundation for the Right to be Born). This center, with its seven national and three international branches, has given refuge to 12,570 women and their babies. Three times the Fundación has blocked the legalization of baby-killing.

With the Universidad de La Salle, the wise Astrid organized the fifth national prolife seminar in Bogotá, which I keynoted. Although 300 had been expected, barely 60 attended. The low numbers may indicate the level of interest.

Then I was to address 300 major seminarians and 400 priests, and to give each one a packet of Spanish-language literature prepared by Magaly Llaguno, the genius who runs HLI's bustling Miami office. Sadly, the date with the seminarians inexplicably fell through, and the priests didn't come. But all the packets were delivered later, and the reaction was most favorable. Also, shortly after I left, Bogotá's Cardinal Mario Revollo Bravo organized a large meeting of priests and heads of organizations to fight the anti-life devil. Please pray for Colombia!

LOCAL BISHOPS FIGHT CONDOMS IN PERU

Alberto Fujimori, president since July 28, is saddling his country with a program of free condoms and abortifacient Pills and IUDs, paid for by a $1.2 million UNFPA (U.N. Fund for Population Activities) grant. Fewer women use contraceptives/abortifacients in Peru than in almost any other Latin American country, just 23 percent. The average mother bears 3.7 children; in the Andes Mountains, 6.3. An estimated one in five pregnancies ends in illegal abortion, more than 100,000 annually for twenty-two million people. Here PP calls itself the "Institute for Responsible Parenthood."

Now all citizens should be "informed of all options so they can freely choose," says the arrogant "Catholic" Fujimori, asserting that the "government does not force anyone." He says he opposes abortion—but for how long?

The bishops are standing firm against Fujimori's massive plan. He accused the Church of having "medieval opinions and a recalcitrant stand" when it comes to fertility control. He scoffed at the bishops' insistence on natural family planning (NFP), calling it unrealistic. In other words, the president, like PP, is saying that human beings are animals that the government must rig with abortifacient drugs, devices, and plugs. (Some U.S. bishops would agree, as we'll see in the next *Report*.)

The Peruvian hierarchy, loyal to Pope John Paul II and Catholic doctrine, told the president that the government should improve education and stimulate the economy, thus lessening unemployment and malnutrition. In a widely publicized statement, the bishops insisted that "development is not acceptable when human and moral values do not have primacy."

For some time we've been doing all we can to help the gallant Peruvian bishops; we're assisting them in preparing a national pastoral. On the Feast of the Annunciation a group of *diputados* (national congressmen) started praying the rosary for life in the national congress; they offer prayers every Tuesday in the Blue Room. Please pray for Peru, too.

98 PERCENT OF ROMANIAN BABIES BEING ABORTED

We're in touch with the recently formed Baptist prolife group in this country and with Baptist leaders: the

Association of Christian Doctors in Romania; Petrus Dugulescu, the pastor of Bethel Baptist Church; Paul Negrut, pastor of the largest Baptist church in Europe; and Vasik Talos, president of the Romanian Evangelical Alliance.

All are appalled by the influx of foreign doctors who are killing their nation's babies. Prolifers there give us the incredible information that 980 out of every 1,000 preborn babies are being destroyed! Another incredible figure: 125,000 orphans, many hundreds of whom are infected with AIDS.

Five days after the dictator Ceausescu's execution last December 27, abortion was legalized. It now costs 30 cents to have a child aborted. Every gynecologist performs dozens of abortions daily. Romania now ranks fourth after Red China, the USSR, and Bulgaria in preborn babies killed per capita. The birthrate is considerably below what is needed for national reproduction.

Last May the Pro-vita Brincoveanu movement was founded; its president is the poet Dr. Ivan Alexandru, a member of parliament. As you read this, our HLI literature and videos are going into the hands of Romanian prolifers from our full-color press in Yugoslavia and from our world headquarters here.

Since 1968, Fr. Marx has spread the pro-life/family message on more than 2,000 talk shows (this one in Belgium.)

Fr. Marx in Onitsha, Nigeria—where the pro-life/family message is as welcome as a new baby.

Hanging on every word, Nigeria's future priests interview Fr. Marx for their seminary's publication.

Sex Ed: An Unnatural Disaster

No. 77   February 1991

Judging from our mail, phone calls, and many
conversations with fine Catholics, the U.S. bishops
truly shot themselves in the foot at their recent
meeting when they approved a secretly produced, barely
discussed set of guidelines for Catholic-school sex
"education." It bears the pretentious title *Human
Sexuality: A Catholic Perspective for Education and
Lifelong Learning.*

A sample of parental complaints we've heard: "Traditional Catholics had better unite and declare war and
actively promote 'No Financial Support for Catholic
Heretics—Bishops Most Particularly.'" "How can the
bishops, who have spent at least $100 million paying for
the crimes of pedophile priests whom they handled badly—
sending them to different, even plush, parishes, while
knowing about their problem—now be guiding us in a
matter where [the popes say] parents have a special
priority?"

A good example of the latter practice is provided by
Archbishop John Roach of St. Paul-Minneapolis. About the
time he admitted he had written the AIDS section of the
guidelines, a court forced him to pay $3.5 million for
knowingly assigning a pedophile priest from another
diocese to one of his own parishes—after he'd received two
warnings from Auxiliary Bishop Robert Carlson, then his
chancellor. In court, Archbishop Roach claimed he had
trusted the advice of a psychiatrist too much. This doctor
told the judge that child molestation wasn't his specialty.

PARENTS SHUT OUT, SEX DISSENTERS WELCOMED

Why was the sex-ed document composed in such secrecy,
by a secret committee, and with virtually no parental
input? Some committee members could hardly have been
disinterested. One was Archbishop Roach's Father John
Forliti, a public dissenter to *Humanae Vitae* and a darling
of the *National Catholic Reporter.* I once examined Father

Forliti's sex-"education" materials, to my dismay; his public school curriculum, *Human Sexuality: Values and Choices,* was approved by pro-abortion, anti-Catholic Planned Parenthood! Enough said.

Father Forliti is the theological consultant on the secular humanist William C. Brown's anti-Magisterium

---

Why was the sex-ed document composed in such secrecy, by a secret committee, and with virtually no parental input?

New Creation series (see *Report No. 60*), which includes a recommended reading list filled with books and authors representing the very dregs of the sexual revolution: Sol Gordon, Wardell Pomeroy, Eric W. Johnson, William A. Black, PP's abortion-pushing Alan Guttmacher, and teen-novelist Judy Blume—all hostile to Catholic morality. Father Forliti was also the director of youth programs for the Minneapolis-based Search Institute, a front for PP.

The treatment of homosexuality in Father Forliti's *Issues in Sexuality,* particularly in the film portions, doesn't reflect Catholic teaching. Produced by the Catholic Education Center of St. Paul and Minneapolis, the series bears the imprimatur of Archbishop Roach, who, by the way, dissented to *Humanae Vitae* in his first meeting with reporters after being elected president of the U.S. bishops in 1980.

Archbishop Roach, who's enamored with the rebel Father Charles Curran's theology, wrote this to the many Catholic parents protesting Father Forliti's productions: "He is an absolutely sound theologian...and enjoys the respect of virtually all of his peers."

Other hardly disinterested members of the secret committee were Coleen Mast, producer and marketer of chastity education manuals, and a recently appointed bishop who has been promoting Benziger's dangerous *Becoming a Person* sex series since 1971. Other committee members are known dissenters to *Humanae Vitae.*

Pleading for more time, the Bridgeport, Connecticut,

Bishop Edward M. Egan complained that he'd been given no time to read the Guidelines; the theologically acute and courageous Bishop Austin Vaughan remarked that this was the first time he had received an embargoed document. Did the bishops vote to approve something they hadn't read? Why the rush to push through an inherently controversial document fraught with the most serious consequences and held secret for two and one-half years?

Astonishingly, in a news conference, Auxiliary Bishop William Newman of Baltimore, chairman of the sex-ed committee, revealed that he didn't even know the pivotal document quoted by virtually every pope since 1929, Pope Pius XI's *Illius Divini Magistri*—a monumental document on Catholic education with an insightful section on sex education.

SHEPHERDS SILENT ON ANTILIFE PRACTICES

Recently a U.S. bishop (whose name I'll withhold for now), presented with the scientific and medical proof that the Pill is an abortifacient, crassly refused to accept this evidence, perhaps because he'd have to tell his people the truth about the Pill.

The U.S. bishops have said nothing explicitly about sterilization, even though some 30 percent of Catholic married couples have neutered ("fixed") themselves. (The *Washington Post* says that in 38 percent of U.S. couples the husband or the wife has been sterilized.)

And make no mistake, the media-hyped new "contraceptive," the surgically implanted, time-capsule Norplant, is actually an abortifacient. The U.S. bishops have been totally silent about it. In Bangladesh and Egypt, poor women had Norplant inserted and tested on them without their informed consent; in Brazil, so many problems occurred that Norplant trials were ended. The *Philadelphia Inquirer* editorially suggested forcing Norplant on the "underclass." A California judge actually coerced a poor woman to use that abortifacient.

You might reasonably expect the National Right to Life

Committee, whose legislative strategy accepts some abortions, to say nothing against this new method of killing unborn life, but surely you'd expect our bishops to protest. Why haven't they?

Columnist Joseph Sobran understated his point: "Officially, Catholic sexual morality hasn't changed a bit. But the American bishops haven't been reaffirming it very vocally lately. They have been *remarkably quiet* throughout the sexual revolution....They have muted their voices when they should have been thundering...[emphasis added]" (The *Washington Times,* 17 November 89).

The harm done by the sex-ed guidelines can be seen from the remarks of the Covington, Kentucky, Bishop William Hughes, as reported in the minutes of his priests' senate: "Sex education—This was directed to the leadership in the diocese as they prepare programs. It was excellent, pas-torally sensitive. The section relative to birth control is done in fidelity to the Magisterium but with great understanding of the lack of acceptance among people."

According to our records, Bishop Hughes is very weak on abortion. In 1984, in a signed document, he complained that abortion was given "too much emphasis." Compare this complaint with Pope John Paul II's admonition to all Americans upon his departure from the USA in 1987: "That is the dignity of America, the reason she exists, the condition of her survival, yes, the ultimate test of her greatness: to respect every human person, especially the weak and most defenseless ones, those as yet unborn."

Compare it, also, with Cardinal John O'Connor's statements at the North American College in Rome on 28

Cardinal John O'Connor: "Abortion has become the no. 1 challenge for the Church in the United States.... The entire credibility and authority of the faith is at stake."

November 1990: "Abortion has become the no. 1 challenge for the Church in the United States....What's important once life goes?...The entire credibility and authority of the faith is at stake."

Bishop Hughes has also sponsored notorious pro-abort speakers in his diocese: Rosemary Ruether, Father Robert Drinan, Marlo Thomas, the state senator Ernesto Scorsone, and more. Northern Right to Life of Kentucky, under the sterling leadership of the lawyer Robert Cetrulo, seems finally to have goaded Bishop Hughes into forming a diocesan prolife commission, after the abortionists have killed twenty-six million babies.

HOW CAN PILL USERS TEACH CATHOLIC MORALITY?

To their credit, by no means all of the bishops voted for the deadly guidelines. For those who did, I have two questions. One, is there a morally neutral sex "education"? (Of course not, because all sexual activity is inherently moral [that is, governed by moral precepts] activity with enormous consequences, as this age should know; in public schools, which most Catholic children attend, religion, morality, and God may not be taught.) And, two, do the bishops really expect "Catholic" school teachers, some 80 percent of whom are contracepting/sterilized/aborted, to be capable of fostering chastity, which should be the chief purpose of so-called sex education?

As a former teacher, I simply cannot imagine a contracepting or neutered teacher's conveying to children the subtle nuances of Christian sexuality, which will forever remain a mystery—like the human personality itself, which sexuality pervades. Such teachers cannot inspire or generate a loving chastity in young people who've been victimized by an utterly corrupt, sex-playing culture. Allow me to borrow the old cliché, "Religion is more caught than taught." That's even more true of teaching chastity! Watch for the home-schooling movement to expand after our bishops' latest blunder.

Furthermore, most Catholic students today attend public schools, many of which provide condom-dispensing machines, "AIDS-prevention" programs, sex "clinics," and PP-trained teachers. In so many words, the bishops' guidelines actually advise Catholics to improve those public-school sex courses!

There's a good deal of the old heresy of Pelagianism (with its denial of original sin and over-reliance on free will) in the episcopal guidelines. They say virtually nothing about original sin and its consequences, the need to avoid occasions of sin, and the absolute necessity of attaining divine grace through prayer, the sacraments, and a reasonable self-denial.

Dr. James Dobson and Gary Bauer, co-authors of *Children at Risk,* note that the secular-humanist agenda promoted by the public-school sexologists can be summed up in this four-point plan:

1. "Provide 'value-free' guidance on sexuality to teenagers."

2. "Provide unlimited quantities of contraceptives to adolescents, dispensed aggressively from clinics located on junior and senior high-school campuses. In so doing, a powerful statement is made to teenagers about adult approval of premarital sexual activity."

3. "Keep parents out of the picture by every means possible."

4. "Provide unlimited access to free abortions for young women who become pregnant; again, *without parental involvement or permission* [emphasis added]."

"A GENERATION OF PERVERTS"

As the Jewish psychiatrist Melvin Anchell insisted recently, classroom sex "education" is producing a generation of perverts. The compulsory AIDS "education" in our schools is heavily influenced by the militant homosexual lobby; it will teach children that homosexual acts are normal or even desirable. The New York City Board of Education is negotiating with homosexual groups, some members of which are already teaching anal intercourse in New York public schools. In a full-page ad in the *New York Times* on 7 January 1991, Gay Men's Health Crisis called for AIDS (i.e., sodomy and fornication) "education" from kindergarten through twelfth grade.

After a lifetime of research and study, the renowned child psychologist, the late Bruno Bettelheim, insisted that "sex education is impossible in the classroom." The famous

Russian convert, Tatiana Goritscheva, maintains, "I believe that this devilish sex education is more dangerous than any atheism. It destroys the personality by destroying the sense of decency...; it also destroys love by separating the physical from the spiritual."

The followers of PP's abortion-pushing president, Dr. Alan Guttmacher, asked him whether the battle for legal abortion had finally been won after the 1973 *Roe v. Wade* decision that gave the USA abortion-on-demand through all nine months of pregnancy. Guttmacher urged them not "to discharge the troops" because "only sex education in every school would insure ultimate victory." The U.S. bishops blundered into PP's trap.

Who advises our hapless bishops? In the instruction *The Ecclesial Vocation of the Theologian,* Cardinal Joseph Ratzinger reminded them,"The pastoral task of the Magisterium is one of vigilance." Our should-be shepherds have generally failed us.

Recently a group of lay people formed the Alliance for Chastity Education (ACE, P.O. Box 11297, Cincinnati, Ohio 45211-0297). It remains to be seen how they'll be able to promote chaste living in faith-ignorant young people by means of only one or two talks, considering how sensitive, personal, and intimate this area is. But I wish them every success.

SOME QUESTIONS FOR THE BISHOPS

It won't do for the bishops to explain that parents who object to sex lessons can withdraw their children from those classes. Sex "education" or "family-life education" is often strewn through the whole curriculum, not confined to just one class.

If the bishops' sex-ed course represents good Catholic teaching, why are parents allowed to deprive their kids of it? And if it *isn't* good Catholic teaching, why are the bishops putting it into Catholic schools?

Besides, what curiosities do you build into a child who has been withdrawn by parents from a sex-ed class? Imagine the after-class discussions between the kids who were allowed in and those who weren't. Can't the bishops see that the "enlightened," experienced children will "teach" the children who were kept out? And won't the "cool" kids make fun of the "nerds" who have such "out-of-it" parents?

Why would the bishops want to exclude the parents from such vital education/formation when all of the

---

What curiosities do you build into a child who has been withdrawn by parents from a sex-ed class?

---

immoral, secular sex-ed programs do precisely that? Consider the beautiful innocence of an unsuspecting young child in his natural "latency period." When adults force explicit sexual details on the child prematurely, they may do lifelong damage. I know "Catholic" schools where fourth-graders are faced with "fertility awareness." *New Creation* teaches fifth-graders how to stimulate female genitalia. Why?

In forty-three years of priesthood, I've done my share of trying to teach human sexuality and chastity. Today, more than ever, I'm totally convinced that education in this area of life belongs in the home, with the parents; if offered in a truly Catholic school, it must always remain under parents' strict guidance and exist with their permission, as all papal documents have insisted. Every priest who deals much with young Catholics knows how fast the spiritual life dries up and religion becomes a straitjacket when vulnerable young people become "sexually active."

Some say that many or most parents neglect their children's sexual education. It's easy to assume this neglect. But if parents really do fail to teach their kids, why don't we teach the parents to teach them? Besides, if the parents are living a truly Catholic life that stems from adequate catechetics and thorough preparation for the marital vocation, they won't fail to teach their children—by example.

HOW TO SAVE KIDS FROM SEX ED

Virtually every day here at HLI headquarters, we receive reports and materials from good parents, teachers, priests, and nuns revealing what's being taught in both "Catholic" and public schools. Some of these materials are so raw and offensive that I choose not to show them to all staff members.

Because I'm a good-bishop-affirmer and not a bishop-basher, I can only conclude that our bishops don't know what's going on in this crucial area. Under the noses of our best bishops and in our best dioceses, there are activities in "Catholic" schools that would shock the most "progressive" of our episcopal leaders.

In the light of what we know and have seen, we can only urge good parents who wish to raise their precious children properly to utterly reject and resist the bishops'

I can only conclude that our bishops don't know what's going on in this crucial area.

---

school sex-education guidelines; the bishops didn't mandate their directives.

The three most urgent things the prelates could do are to strongly reassert traditional sexual morality as embodied in *Humanae Vitae;* to clean up the Catholic educational curriculum and CCD (Confraternity of Christian Doctrine) program (which, if properly taught by truly Catholic teachers, would promote virtuous living and particularly chastity, the most ignored virtue in modern life); and to replace the anti-Magisterium people on their diocesan and USCC staffs with men and women loyal to Rome's teachings.

I've seen sex-"education" programs in many countries of the world. I challenge any bishop, educator, priest, nun, or layman anywhere to prove to me that organized classroom sex education has worked anywhere.

CARDINAL & BISHOPS LOBBY FOR "GAYS"

Astonishingly, the assembled bishops proved to be less concerned about offending parents and violating parental rights than about offending homosexuals. Auxiliary Bishop Peter Rosazza of Hartford said the pastoral guidance from the Congregation for the Doctrine of the Faith in Rome had caused "untold harm" to homosexuals and that homosexuals would "find it offensive."

San Francisco's Archbishop John Quinn said the Congregation's statement was "correct," but that he worried it would be interpreted to mean that "homosexuality is bad."

What did he think the next day, when the *San Francisco Chronicle* ran the headline "U.S. Catholic Bishops Say Homosexuality Is Not a Sin"? How many sodomites took this statement to mean that homosexual *acts* weren't sinful? How many used it to seduce youngsters?

After reaching an impasse, Cardinal Joseph Bernardin, Chicago's master compromiser, came to the rescue. He said he found himself "on the horns of a dilemma," wanting to be faithful to the Congregation but also sensitive to the needs of homosexuals. So, at his suggestion, the "offensive" phrase in the Congregation's document was relegated to a footnote with an explanatory text by Archbishop Quinn. Cardinal Bernardin, Archbishop Quinn, and others objected to Rome's statement because it said even the inclination to homosexuality "must be seen as an objective disorder."

The rebel bishop of Saginaw, Michigan, Kenneth Untener, who likes to be called "Ken," shot himself in both feet. Despite Pope John Paul II's repeated insistence that *Humanae Vitae* is a settled matter, not open to theological discussion, "Ken" brazenly suggested that the bishops reopen the whole question of contraception. The Church's credibility on abortion is at stake if they don't do so, Ken declared.

William E. McManus, the retired bishop of Fort Wayne-South Bend, chimed in, "The [bishops'] agenda was distant from the anxieties and hopes of people back home....If this trend to talk from the top down continues, we will not be heard because we have not listened."

"Ken" and Bishop McManus, like many bishops, obviously don't understand the interconnected, spreading, developing contraception-sterilization-abortion-infanticide-euthanasia syndrome. According to our investigations, neither prelate has promoted NFP, thus having done virtually nothing to help the unhappy Catholic couples they cite. Bishop McManus once told three mothers who complained that contraception was being taught in his Catholic high schools, "Oh well, they'll practice it anyway."

Appealing to the *sensus fidelium* (the mind/sense of the faithful), Ken of Saginaw asserted, "When people disagree with us, we cannot simply assume that it is mere opinion." But since when are the faithful wiser than twenty centuries of the Holy Spirit's guiding His Church, and the conviction, solemnly proclaimed again and again, that contraception is "intrinsically evil" (Popes Pius XI, Pius XII, John XXIII, John Paul I, and John Paul II) or "intrinsically dishonest" (Pope Paul VI).

Amazingly, the free-wheeling Ken, who has been known to address official Church meetings dressed in sport shirt and slacks, seemed impressed by a confidential poll he took of twenty-three members of his advisory diocesan council, to whom he presented the section of the guidelines dealing with the Church's teaching on contraception. Twenty-two said they had serious questions about Church doctrine on birth control.

Now, how many of them practice contraception or early abortion? Are they thoroughly schooled in NFP? Do they know the ravages that contraceptives/abortifacients/sterilization/abortion have inflicted on society and Church in the West? Has Ken explained to them the connection between sinful birth control and abortion—how the foresight of contraception has led to the hindsight of abortion everywhere?

If the twenty-three are typically "good Catholics," as Ken proclaims, 80 percent are or have been practicing contraception. The famous British Anglican gynecologist Ian Donald told me, "As one lives, so one thinks." I offer this observation for Ken's meditation.

By the way, when Ken was rector of St. John's provincial seminary in Detroit, he introduced pornographic movies as educational tools for his seminarians, who presumably could then better oppose or handle pornography. When this custom came to light, reliable sources tell me, Ken's appointment as bishop was suspended—until Detroit's Archbishop John Cardinal

Dearden (of "Call to Action" fame) went to Rome to rescue the appointment. Alas, said the prophet, "My people are destroyed for lack of knowledge" (Hosea 4:6).

A MASSIVE APOSTASY

Another strangely secret meeting was "The Wisdom of Women," a 29 November-2 December 1990 symposium held in Arlington, Virginia, sponsored by the Bishops' Committee on Women in Society and the Church, of which the Rochester, New York, Bishop Matthew Clark is chairman. Typically, the keynoter Bishop Clark chose five issues "which cause tension in the Church today": birth control, abortion, celibacy, women's ordination, and selection of bishops.

Never mind that Pope John Paul II long ago asked the bishops to quiet the talk about women priests; never mind that he's said the Church's teaching on contraception is a settled issue! And you'll recall that the recent synod on the priesthood in Rome reaffirmed the value and validity of celibacy. The selection of bishops is, naturally, a sore point with rebel theologians and their bishops, because the pope tries not to appoint their kind—thanks be to God!

Bishop Clark proclaimed, "To declare a matter closed does not...stop the questioning of the faithful." That's true, Bishop Clark, as long as bishops like you and your wayward theologians disobey the Supreme Pontiff and keep fomenting rebellion. We know your game.

We in the USA and Canada are witnessing a massive apostasy, from (some) bishops on down; with more than fifteen million fallen-aways, we're undergoing a total spiritual/moral crisis. As Cardinal Edouard Gagnon has said, the U.S. Church has already succumbed to moral schism. Cardinal Joseph Ratzinger has observed that the problem of the Church in the Western world is the problem of the bishops' not obeying the pope and not teaching the whole faith.

Please pray that our bishops defend their sheep.

What safer place for this Nigerian baby than in the arms of a prolife missionary?

Fr. Marx and theologian Fr. John Hardon, SJ, at HLI's Tenth World Conference on Love, Life and the Family in Santa Clara, California in 1991.

Sr. Lucille Durocher, President of HLI Canada, with one of her favorite people.

"Don't forget about me!" says two-year old Brian Stong.

Ardent prolife activist Matthias Selemobri was one of 13 missionary priests ordained on 22 June 1991 at the Missionary Seminary of St. Paul, Nigeria.

Bratislava Cathedral resounds with prayer from main celebrant Josef Cardinal Tomko and Slovakian bishops in 1990. HLI's symposium in Bratislava, Czechoslovakia drew 1,500 participants from Eastern and Central Europe.

The long and the short of it: Enni Banda from Zambia and longtime friend and supporter Anthony Boone at our Eighth Annual World Conference in Miami in 1990.

Archbishop Angelo Fernandes of New Delhi and Fr. Ray Mulhern in HLI's chapel.

Prolife apostles Dr. and Mrs. Claude Newbury with their maid and Fr. Marx at the Newbury home in Johannesburg, South Africa.

In Costa Rica, Fr. Marx shows the president's wife dangerous stuff: IPPF sex education texts.

Your taxes at work destroying the family in Nigeria.

Brenda Bonk, Fr. Marx's busy secretary, doing what her boss often does—several things at once.

Now Playing at the Cathedral

No. 78   March 1991

People don't like to hear the words "I told you so." But for years, HLI has been telling the world unpalatable truths that you see more and more about in the news today. For example, you'll recall that for more than a decade I've sounded warnings about the worldwide Moslem resurgence known as "the Islamic Revival."

LET'S ELIMINATE CHRISTIANITY

In the summer of 1990, twenty-four of Africa's fifty-one governments founded the Islam in Africa Organization (IAO), based in Lagos, Nigeria's biggest city. The goal of IAO is to annihilate all other religions in Africa, particularly Christianity. Strangely, nothing about this intention has appeared in the USA's secular or Catholic press. Nigeria is the world's largest black country and has a Moslem military government. Last year this oil-rich nation gave the Moslems $16 billion to propagate Islam around the world.

Another leader in the IAO is resource-rich but under-developed Sudan, Africa's geographically largest country. Today this immense, well-watered land suffers from a Moslem military government and from a Moslem civil war against the Christians and the followers of the traditional African animist religion. I'll have more for you on the Moslems in a future Report.

WE TOLD YOU SO

HLI also exposed Bishop Joseph Ferarrio's mess in the Diocese of Honolulu. Two years later the bishops of the USA, meeting in Baltimore, caught a shocking glimpse of a Bishop Ferrario scandal we could only hint at. Since then the Catholic press has published more and more horror stories from the island diocese.

The euthanasia threat, highlighted by the starvation-killing of Nancy Cruzan, didn't come upon our society overnight. In September 1970 an ominous editorial in

California Medicine spoke of "a new ethic" of "birth selection" and "death selection." In 1971 I published one of the first warnings of the inevitable mercy killing to come, *The Mercy Killers,* which sold more than two million copies in various editions. *Doorways to Death* is an enlarged and revised edition to be published soon.

You'll recall, also, that for years HLI has pointed out that there is a significant connection between contraception and abortion, that contraception is not a remedy for abortion and that not one nation with widespread contraception has ever avoided legalizing abortion. Having visited eighty-two countries, I can find no exception; nor has anyone else been able to.

Today, at last, more and more people seem to be seeing this deadly relationship, including many good prolife Protestants—especially Randy Terry, the great rescue leader. He keeps telling Christians they shouldn't use chemical or mechanical birth control. Incidentally, Lutherans for Life have done what the Catholic bishops have yet to do: warned their people that the Pill and IUD are abortifacients.

For more than a decade HLI has tried to alert the whole West, and especially its Church leaders, to the disastrous consequences of low birthrates that result from sterile and immoral sexual practices before, within, and outside of marriage. Now you read articles about how the Japanese, the Canadians, the Singaporeans, the Western Europeans (particularly the Germans, the Italians, the Austrians, and the French), and everyone behind the crumpled curtain (except the Poles and the Russians) are becoming frantic about their relatively baby-less nations and the invasion of uneducated immigrants, many of them Moslems. Recently the U.S. Congress agreed to accept 750,000 immigrants annually into the USA; Canada, with a population ten times smaller, will take in 250,000. More than half a million illegals also invade the USA every year.

No nation in modern times has been able to significantly repair a birthrate ruined by the immoral sexual habits promoted by Planned Parenthood (PP), by foundations such as Ford and Hewlett-Packard, by the news media and the government—and more than tolerated

by the weak bishops and rebel theologians of the dying
countries. The 4.1 million babies born in 1990 still leave
the average U.S. family with barely two offspring (we need
2.4 babies per family for national survival).

I keep saying and writing that perhaps never in
history has it been more evident that the Catholic Church
was right all along about sexual morality and the essential

**The Church was right all along about
sexual morality and the essential role
of chastity.**

---

role of chastity. As the old saying goes, God always
forgives, people sometimes forgive, but nature never
forgives. Nature is jealous of her fertility; her yea is yea,
and her nay is nay. She will not be mocked or played with;
she strikes back, as anyone who has eyes to see should
know. Ignore the ancient rules and you pay an enormous
price—always.

Part of this price is AIDS, which has already killed
100,000 Americans. AIDS is destroying nations in Africa
and is becoming more and more a heterosexual problem in
the West. Here, it's a dragon to be slain by condoms—one
of many forms of birth control that most U.S. bishops and
virtually all priests staunchly refuse to condemn from
their pulpits, despite having been ordered to do so by Pope
Paul VI's monumental, prophetic 1968 encyclical,
Humanae Vitae. Imagine: Two years ago, the admini-
strative council of the U.S. hierarchy—some fifty bishops,
including a cardinal—was ready to inform Catholic youth
about condoms as a way to avoid AIDS!

At the seventh international meeting of the Society for
the Advancement of Contraception in Singapore last
November, research scientists reported that ten studies of
HIV infection, all involving condom use, revealed a 43
percent chance of getting the fatal HIV infection if one's
"partner" is already afflicted. According to the same report,
condoms prevented the transmission of gonorrhea and
syphilis 57 percent of the time, at most.

A report in the 21 May 1987 *New England Journal of
Medicine* said that "condoms failed to prevent HIV

transmission in 3 of 18 [married] couples, suggesting that
the rate of condom failure with HIV may be as high as 17
percent." Those are the same odds you face playing
Russian roulette. Providing youngsters with condoms is
like making sure that drunk drivers wear seat belts. And
now the New York City Board of Education wants to
distribute condoms to all ninth through twelfth graders. It
defeated a resolution not to teach anal intercourse in
classrooms. The new paganism has gone mad!

SCANDAL AND VIOLENCE DESECRATE A CATHEDRAL

Plainclothes policemen violently assaulted a group of
peaceful, praying prolife Catholics and ejected them from
the Cathedral of the Blessed Sacrament in Sacramento,
California, on 6 January 1991. The desecration took place
during an ecumenical inaugural event honoring the
militantly pro-abort Governor-elect Pete Wilson and his
pro-abort second wife, Gayle.

Two weeks before, on December 23, prolife Catholics
were dismayed to read in the Sacramento Union that their
cathedral was to be turned over (during the time of the
scheduled 10 a.m. Sunday Mass) for one of the events of
Wilson's $2 million inaugural bash. Wilson had asked the
diocese for use of the cathedral.

(As a U.S. Senator, Wilson cosponsored the "Freedom
of Choice Act" of 1989 to make abortion the law of the land
even if the Supreme Court overturns *Roe v. Wade*. He
promised the abortion industry that, as governor, he'd
appoint pro-abort judges, push school sex "clinics," and
give millions more to PP, which operates some twenty
abortoriums in California, including a large one in
Sacramento. He has actively courted California's militant
homosexuals.)

Prolife activist Paul Laubacher immediately wrote to
Monsignor James Kidder, pastor of the cathedral, pleading
with him not to turn it over to Wilson on a Sunday morning;
doing so, Laubacher said, would give people the impression
that Catholics accepted pro-abort politicians and that prolife

protests against Wilson were "really out of step."

Two days later, Albin Rhomberg, director of the Center for Documentation of the American Holocaust, spoke with Sacramento's Bishop Francis Quinn. The prelate defended his decision to let Wilson use the cathedral. "We're not honoring him," said the bishop. "It's the office." Later he asserted, "There are good people on both sides."

As more outrage over Bishop Quinn's decision developed, an *ad hoc* Anti-Desecration League (ADL) was formed. Prolife Christians called and wrote to Monsignor Kidder, Bishop Quinn, all the bishops of California, Cardinal John O'Connor of New York and Archbishop Agostino Cacciavillan, the Vatican pro-nuncio in Washington, DC. They also asked Cardinal Joseph Ratzinger to bring the matter to the attention of Pope John Paul II.

PRIESTS INSULT PROLIFERS

On New Year's Day, Laubacher and Rhomberg met with Monsignor Kidder and an "enormously hostile" Father Charles McDermott to express growing prolife concern about the scandal expected to arise from the Wilson event. They learned that Bishop Quinn had been invited to take part and that presumably the media would feature photos of Bishop Quinn welcoming the Wilsons to the cathedral. (The Associated Press did, in fact, distribute a photo of a cordial handshake between the bishop and Wilson, with a beaming Gayle between them.) The prolifers' pleas met with insults and rejection.

The next day, January 2, Wilson launched a new attack on preborn children. He said he'd appoint State Senator John Seymour to take over Wilson's U.S. Senate seat. Ex-Catholic Seymour had switched from prolife to pro-death to run for lieutenant governor in the June 1990 primary, but had lost. Wilson thus chose a loser who had been repudiated by his own Republican Party, as a reward to the pro-aborts.

Two days later, the *Union* ran a front-page story about prolife opposition to the takeover of the cathedral. It quoted Rhomberg: "This event would more appropriately be held at an abortion clinic." The ADL redoubled its efforts, but to no avail. Bishop Quinn was in Florida on vacation and was said to be unreachable, even by his secretary, until late Saturday night.

The ADL informed Wilson that if he took over the cathedral its members would follow the Holy Father's words and "stand up" for life in the face of such a desecration. An appeal was made on Saturday, January 5, to the bishops of California, assembled in the Los Angeles area for their annual retreat.

POLICE DOGS IN THE SANCTUARY

Efforts to persuade Church officials and Wilson to avert the scandal continued into Sunday morning. A group of Catholics went to the 8 a.m. Mass and stayed afterward to pray. The media were told that they intended to stay in the cathedral to pray and would invoke the right of holy sanctuary against any attempt to eject them. Security agents, wanting the cathedral cleared, actually brought large dogs into the sanctuary to sniff around the altar before the Blessed Sacrament.

The cathedral, only a block from the state capitol, now took on the appearance of an abortion mill expecting a rescue. Yellow plastic "crime scene" police tape was strung

---

Catholics who came for the 10 a.m.
Mass were shunted off to a basement
room by Young Republicans.

---

about the area to funnel ticket-holders into one entrance. (Catholics had to obtain tickets from Wilson to get into their own cathedral!) Police cars blocked nearby streets; and mounted police, SWAT teams, and paddy wagons were drawn up near the bishop's residence. Catholics who came for the 10 a.m. Mass were shunted off to a basement room by Young Republicans. Mass was offered in this catacomb.

Police lined the side aisles, and Wilson's ticket-holders, estimated to number 1,200, began entering. So did prolife Catholic ticket-holders such as Joe Scheidler from Chicago and others from California. The Wilsons and senator-designate Seymour took places of honor at the right front.

"WE'RE IN YOUR CHURCH!"

Also present was the director of Planned Parenthood and California's number one abortionist, Edward Allred, who operates some forty abortion centers in California and Chicago. Allred, who makes no secret of his anti-Hispanic prejudice, has killed 1.4 million babies. He's a major Republican Party contributor. The audience of bejeweled and befurred "country-club Republicans" contrasted with the usual Sunday Mass-goers, who are mostly poor and elderly residents of run-down, downtown Sacramento. One pro-abort taunted prolifers, saying, "We're in your church!"

The clergy, including Bishop Quinn, an Episcopal priestess, a rabbi who was to give the sermon, and a Buddhist "acting abbot," were about to proceed up the center aisle. Monsignor Kidder asked the prolife Catholics in the front two pews to move. They refused. Soon they rose and began to pray the Lord's Prayer loudly. To their surprise, all 1,200 people rose with them, including the Wilsons, but didn't pray. Soon the ushers gestured the crowd to sit down, leaving the prolife Catholics standing, still praying the Lord's Prayer.

At this development, Wilson's chief aide, Bob White, who's said to be a Catholic, darted in front of the Wilsons and apparently gave the order unleashing violent assaults on prolife Catholics. Several men roughly began to pull 81-year-old, white-haired John Szabo from his pew. Because Mr. Szabo has had quadruple-bypass heart surgery, his daughter, Theresa Reali, who had been praying silently nearby, rose to caution the men. They left him and roughly grabbed Theresa, a Third Order Carmelite and mother of four children, and dragged her behind a large pillar.

JUST FOLLOWING THE BISHOP'S ORDERS?

She told them she wanted to pray and to take sanctuary in the cathedral. They said Bishop Quinn had ordered the removal. Then, holding her hands so that she couldn't protect herself, they dropped her on her head on the hard floor. She cried out in excruciating pain but was dragged to a side door in a semi-conscious state. Outside, Sacramento police grabbed her, cuffed her hands in a painful position behind her back, and pulled her away. A friend, Jay Baggett, found that Theresa didn't even recognize him when he spoke to her; afterward, she had no memory of seeing him or being dragged one block to a temporary prison.

The police rudely threatened Baggett and warned him away, but he insisted they get medical help for Theresa. They made a call on the radio, but a mocking response came back, saying Theresa was "retarded." She received no medical attention despite suffering from severe pain, nausea, and dizziness. Her hands and wrists, still cuffed, went numb as she cried out from the pain in her bruised and wrenched arms and shoulders. A blood blister formed on her left wrist.

Theresa's rosary was still tangled in her numb fingers. A police sergeant who said he was an atheist mocked her Catholic faith, abusing her with foul language. He said she'd need his permission to cry in pain, as he menaced her with his club, slapping it on his palm. After about an hour and a half, the police took Theresa to jail, booked her, and released her.

Her husband, who'd been watching their children, took Theresa to the hospital. Besides a severe head injury, she suffered painful bruises and sprains of her arms, wrists, and body. Two days later she underwent a brain scan and a month later was still being treated by a neurologist for head pains and dizziness.

PROLIFERS BRUTALIZED AS REPUBLICANS APPLAUD

After Theresa was brutalized, three men assaulted her elderly father, who was still kneeling in a front pew (he only learned of her head injury later). They pulled him out of the pew and dragged him across the entire front of the cathedral, injuring his back, arms, and wrist. His rosary, a precious gift from his deceased wife, was torn to pieces and scattered. Then his son Richard, a retired peace officer, was similarly assaulted and dragged out.

Scott Kiley, a young friend of the Szabos, suffered serious bruises and injuries to his arms and body when he was wrestled out. Two men grabbed Al Rhomberg and dragged him to the center aisle and up to the altar while he shouted, "Sanctuary! Holy sanctuary!" He was roughly dragged between some pews, injuring his arms and knees, and then dumped on the concrete outside. Charles Shunk, Nell Keim, Dr. John Byrnes, and his brother Michael were also ejected. The audience applauded.

Police locked the prolifers in a paddy wagon that was reeking with puddles of vomit. When the prisoners shouted, "Long live Christ the King," the paddy wagon moved near the bishop's house; it seemed to be a command post for the Wilson staff, who apparently had taken over the whole church property.

Toward the end of the Wilson event, Joe Scheidler rose in his pew near Wilson and spoke to Monsignor Kidder. Joe said that if no prayers were offered for the preborn babies the proceedings were a sacrilege, not a religious ceremony. He attempted to unroll a banner bearing the word SACRILEGE but was immediately hustled out into the foul-smelling paddy wagon. Six officers tortured him by twisting his arms and bending his thumbs. Finally, as Wilson was exiting down the center aisle, Jack Cook tried to speak to him. He, too, was pounced on, roughly dragged out, and, with his wrist bloodied, locked in the wagon.

The Blessed Sacrament was present at all times.

"HAVE OUR BISHOPS GONE MAD?"

A hundred prolifers picketed outside with signs such as NOW PLAYING AT THE CATHEDRAL: JUDAS AND

"Now playing at the cathedral: Judas and Herod."

HEROD (which appeared on page one of the *Union*), ECUMENICAL MURDER IS STILL MURDER, and HAVE OUR BISHOPS GONE MAD? Bishop Quinn came out and tried to placate the picketers, but they were incensed at the scandalous and brutal desecration. Cries of "Betrayal," "Today you made me ashamed to be Catholic," and "Judas, Judas" came from the picketers and the captives in the paddy wagon. "I'm really on your side," he insisted. His position is that he was trying to convert Wilson to being prolife.

All ten prolife Catholics were charged with "disrupting a religious service," which could bring them six months in jail. They hold that it was the Wilsons, Seymour, Allred, PP, and their pro-abort supporters who disturbed two *real* religious services: the scheduled 10 a.m. Mass and the Catholics' prayer in the cathedral. The ADL believes that the cathedral, desecrated by the scandal and the violent assaults on praying Catholics, must be reconsecrated, just as Cardinal O'Connor reconsecrated St. Patrick's Cathedral after the pro-abort, pro-homosexual desecration of December 1989.

The assaults upon and legal prosecutions of the prolife Catholics are a chilling demonstration of the power of the pro-abortion forces. They can now orchestrate "religious" events in our churches, displace a scheduled Sunday Mass, and even reach into a Catholic cathedral to taunt, assault, torture, eject, and then prosecute prolife Catholics praying there.

Compare Bishop Quinn's policy toward Pete Wilson, who's responsible for the deaths of countless unborn babies, with Pope Pius XI's policy toward Adolf Hitler. When the Nazi head of state visited Rome in 1938, the pontiff closed every Vatican building and retired to his villa at Castel Gandolfo, outside the city, until the antilife politician had left town.

MORE SCANDALS IN SACRAMENTO

But Bishop Quinn's diocese is known for strange goings-on. For example, despite his written denial to me, "Dignity" (homosexual) Masses still take place openly at St. Francis Church in Sacramento, in defiance of Rome's orders. Dignity's newsletter comes out of St. Francis Friary. Father Bill Holland, who celebrates the homosexual Masses, is an assistant pastor at Bishop Quinn's cathedral.

(He was present at the Wilson event, glaring icily at the prolifers.)

The diocese seems to view the cathedral as a hall that's available for hire. It let the American River Nursing College use it for a raucous, secular graduation ceremony. (American River Hospital teaches people to kill unborn babies.) The Blessed Sacrament wasn't removed; a few Catholics maintained a prayer vigil during the proceedings. Concerts have also been given in the cathedral.

Not long ago, Monogue Catholic High School presented a classroom sex-"education" play featuring a girl who lay on her back holding a banana for a boy to put a condom on. There are many other horror stories.

Please send Bishop Quinn a courteous letter about the Wilson sacrilege. He's at 1119 K Street/PO Box 1706, Sacramento, CA 95808. By the way, Al Rhomberg will speak at our world conference in Santa Clara.

ABORTION AND BABY-SAVING IN ISRAEL

In *Special Report No. 34* I detailed the significant leadership role that certain pro-abortion Jews in the USA, Israel, and elsewhere have played in promoting abortion.

I reported that Israel registers one of the highest abortion rates in the world. This nation of 4.8 million people is 16 percent Arab and 13 percent Moslem; the Arabs/Moslems maintain a high birthrate, but the Jewish birthrate is barely at population-replacement level. Leaders in the Knesset (parliament) have admitted that the day may come when non-Jews can outvote the Jews for control of the parliament.

But now, after years of divisive political paralysis, the Israeli government may be dramatically reshaped in the near future by the coveted votes of more than half a million new Israeli citizens from the USSR. So many Soviet Jews are arriving that every six weeks they can elect a new member of the Knesset.

According to the 12 September 1990 *New York Times,* so far that year approximately 150,000 Soviet Jews had entered Israel. Close to 200,000 were expected by January 1 of this year; as many as 400,000 may come in 1991 and a like number in 1992. This influx may help to keep Israel temporarily Jewish.

And now there's more good news: Israeli prolifers have formed a second baby-saving operation, called "Be' ad"— Association for the Protection of the Unborn. Also, limiting abortions was one of the conditions to be met by the Agudath Israel Party (representing the orthodox Jewish minority) in joining a coalition with Prime Minister Yitzhak Shamir's Likud Party.

THEOLOGIANS VS. "PRE-EMBRYOS"

Last summer, after months of serious debate, the British Parliament legalized experiments on preborn humans in the first fourteen days of life. The lawmakers called these fourteen days the "pre-embryo" stage. The chief motivation behind their action was to justify abortifacient pills, devices, and implants (such as Norplant, about which you've been reading so much), as well as to permit experimentation to develop new abortifacients. Of course, everyone knows the experimentation/killing won't be limited to fourteen days.

One of the chief sources the parliamentary enemies of life relied on was the book *When Did I Begin?* by the Australian theologian Father Norman Ford. He argued that we surely can't establish personhood before the fourteenth day, when the new life is fully implanted in the mother's womb.

Now rebellious U.S. theologians and medical ethicists have taken up the cause of killing early humans through the false concept of the "pre-embryo." Among the rebels are Notre Dame's Father Richard McCormick, SJ, whose pseudo-arguments against personhood in the first fourteen days were published by the religious-affairs editor of the New York Times in a long article on 13 January 1991. Others pushing this scientifically false view include the philosopher Father Allan B. Wolter, formerly of the Catholic University of America, and the ethicist Thomas A. Shannon of Massachusetts' Worcester Polytechnic Institute. Dr. Shannon is a charter member of the lying pro-abortion group Catholics for a Free Choice, which receives funds from the pornography industry.

Actually, British scientists have already dropped the

fanciful term "pre-embryo" for fear of ridicule. Now they use "pre-implantation embryo," but Father McCormick and company either haven't caught on yet or refuse to face the truth.

In his fascinating testimony defending the lives of seven frozen embryos stored in a "concentration can" in Tennessee last year, the famous French geneticist Dr. Jerome Lejeune showed that the concept of the "pre-embryo" is a fraud. Using the very latest genetic and other scientific information, he proved that human life begins at conception/fertilization. His brilliant, 72-page testimony has been circulated widely, but if you haven't read it you have a treat awaiting you (you may order your copy from HLI for $3 postpaid).

Now Professor Lejeune has published a 114-page book, *L'Enceinte Concentrationnaire (The Concentration Can, The Latest on Human Beginnings)*,s containing not only the Tennessee testimony but also two additional chapters of information, plus appendices. It's frighteningly important to educate scientists and others to see through the theological mischief of the McCormicks, the McBriens, the Shannons, and their cohorts. (No author can get published in the theological and medical journals to refute their dangerous notions.) We desperately want to publish and distribute Lejeune's masterpiece, but it'll cost about $10,000. It's not possible to exaggerate the importance of this document, and we are begging our friends to contribute any amount they can to its publication.

Robertas Skrinskas, our prolife seminarian in Lithuania, sent proof of growing vocations: future priests attending the major seminary in Kaunas.

Indian madonna and child in Ecuador.

A Mission to Puerto Rico

No. 79   April 1991

The older I get, the more I see that the Vicars of Christ, under the guidance of the Holy Spirit, usually are far ahead in assessing what the world needs. For example, imagine what a different Catholic Church it would be if the bishops of the world had heeded Pope Pius XII's two eloquent pleas for the development and teaching of natural family planning (NFP) in 1951, almost a decade before the advent of the Pill.

FOLLOW THE POPE!

In those documents, the celibate pope showed the depth of his knowledge about the inner workings of marriage. His many weekly talks to newlyweds also demonstrated his insight. In the two statements on NFP, the Holy Father spoke about the legitimacy of "birth regulation," as compared with the hideous, inhuman "birth control"—a term he, in fact, studiously avoided.

In his second allocution to the Large Family Association of Italy, Pius praised the parents for their courage and generosity in begetting numerous children for God. He reminded them that the large family has often been the "seedbed" of religious vocations. But, said the wise pontiff, the Church understands all of marriage, and there will always be couples who, for various reasons, cannot have many offspring.

In fact, continued the pope, he could think of couples who, given their situations, would, through natural methods, responsibly avoid pregnancy altogether, expressing their marital love in intercourse only during the God-given infertile times. (He didn't specify the situations he had in mind, but we can all think of some.) In God's Providence, such couples had "a special vocation" to serve the family and Church in other ways, the pope observed.

When I was ordained in 1947, NFP was already a viable method of birth regulation, although by no means as effective as today's developed methods. For the knowledgeable and motivated couple, these natural methods have proven as effective as any contraceptive or

---

For the knowledgable and motivated couple, these natural methods have proven as effective as any contraceptive or abortiacient.

---

abortifacient, outranked only by sterilization. (For proof, send $2 to HLI and ask for "The Effectiveness of NFP.")

How different our contracepting-sterilizing-aborting-euthanizing selfish world would be today if all the bishops had obeyed the pope, had made NFP a requirement in all marriage-preparation courses, and had taught against the monstrosity of artificial birth control, as the Church has done for twenty centuries! Nor did Catholic universities and scientists obey Pope Pius XII when he pleaded with them to conduct research to perfect human, natural methods.

If they had done this research, a good portion of the world's Catholic couples would be practicing generous parenthood by means of NFP by now. Contracepting or sterilized couples wouldn't be giving scandal to their children and neighbors by brazenly ignoring what the Catholic Church has always taught and what, in fact, our Protestant brethren taught for more than 400 years. Our separated Christian brethren would be witnessing the beautiful family life and love of generous, happy Catholic twosomes; they'd be discovering even faster that immoral and unhealthful contraceptives/abortifacients/sterilization/abortion aren't the answers to the birth-regulation problem.

Is this speculation a form of dreaming? Well, is what we have today better—empty seminaries, boarded-up Catholic schools, dying convents, vacant confessionals, record divorces, pandemic VD, the deadly AIDS plague, fornicating teenagers, two and one-half million couples living together as shackmates, militant homosexuals, and dying nations and churches in the West?

IT'S NOT NICE TO FOOL MOTHER NATURE

Modern contraception has hit a dead end, wrote the contraception/abortion-pushing *New York Times* (12 December 1990). Today people are rejecting the abortifacient Pill and IUD. There's resistance to the impractical, dangerous abortifacient Norplant and the injectible abortifacient Depo-Provera (so dangerous it's banned in the USA). A $2.3 billion fund had to be set up for women injured by the Dalkon Shield, and the contraception field is filled with lawsuits. These factors, says the *Times*, have produced "an unwitting coalition of longtime adversaries— manufacturing companies, courtroom litigators, feminists, right-to-life groups, and religious activists, including the Catholic Church"—resulting in a "birth-control backlash."

We commend the frankness of Stanford University's alert scientist Carl Djerassi, chief developer of the Pill, who presented a possible solution: research on a "jet-age rhythm method which would enable couples to select a method with no adverse side effects." (Planned Parenthood, please note: there *are* adverse effects.) We congratulate him on his late awakening but also remind him that he's forty years behind Pope Pius XII!

What astonishes me is that prolife Protestants are beginning to see that contraception *is* the gateway to abortion because it's a gross abuse of God's exquisite gift of human sexuality. They're realizing, also, that if one can separate the unitive from the procreative aspect of marital intercourse, then unmarried people will be much more inclined to "live together" and teens will be much more likely to fornicate—to mention only two of the many evils. (According to the last newsletter of the American College of Obstetrics and Gynecology, 40 percent of all U.S. abortions in 1990 were performed on the babies of girls fifteen to nineteen years old.)

If Catholic bishops, priests, scientists, and lay people had done their duty, by now our Protestant brethren would be seeing more clearly what a mistake it was when the Anglicans' Lambeth Conference (1930), in a highly disputed decision after a decade of arguing, voted to "tolerate" (note the term) contraception—for the first time in twenty centuries of Christianity.

Last year Randy Terry, the great Protestant rescue leader, told 1,000 adults in Nashville, Tennessee (not known for its Catholicism), that Christians should not use artificial birth control; there wasn't even a whisper of protest.

Dr. Jerome Lejeune, the great French geneticist and member of the Pontifical Academy of Science, once told me that if there was one instance in his life when he felt the Holy Spirit touched the pope and directed him into the right way, it was in issuing *Humanae Vitae.* Had the pope decided wrongly, it would have been the end of the Catholic Church. I shall go to my grave wondering why so many theologians and bishops haven't seen the wisdom of that document and taught it vigorously. But then, no one is so blind as he who will not see.

Another example of profound papal wisdom and providential guidance was Pope Pius XII's remark of 24 August 1939, warning European leaders what a tragedy it would be to go to war: "Nothing is lost with peace. But everything can be lost with war!" How right he was! Little, really, was settled by World War II. The whole of Eastern Europe fell to Communism, from which it's desperately trying to extricate itself now. More than sixty million people lost their lives in that war, to say nothing of the staggering material destruction. And the seeds of future wars were sown.

Now our present great pope (to whom even Mikhail Gorbachev, in a weak moment, gave credit for the breakup of Eastern European Communism) has delivered a similar

---

With one of every four human beings destined soon to be Moslem, what hostile fallout will descend upon Christians around the world?

---

unheeded warning to the world: "War is an adventure with no return." We're already seeing the prophetic wisdom of that remark. Let not the euphoria of "victory" deceive you. With one of every four human beings destined soon to be Moslem, what hostile fallout will descend upon Christians around the world? Remember, in the eyes of the followers of Mohammed *all* non-Moslems are "infidels."

WILL WE LISTEN THIS TIME?

In his recent and longest encyclical, *Redemptoris Missio*, Pope John Paul II pleaded for worldwide Catholic (note: not just Christian) evangelism, even in Moslem countries where it's outlawed and punished. In this encyclical, the pope wrote that the most painful difficulties facing the Church's missionary effort are those in the divided Church itself: the dramatic drop in new priests, the loss of religious practice and values in historically Christian countries, the contracepting/aborting/sterilized couples, the theological confusion, the infighting among Christians, and the friction between fundamentalists and Catholics.

Think of the number of times in the Old Testament that God used hostile nations to bring His wayward chosen people to repentance! Will the Lord of love and life use the proliferating Moslems to punish the many lukewarm Catholics/Christians of the wealthy West? As the old saying goes, if there's one thing we learn from history it's that we learn nothing from history—and surely not much from prophetic, Heaven-sent popes.

So often people ask me when God will strike the nations for their massive babykilling. If the questioner is from the USA, I answer, How much more punishment can there be, when seminaries are virtually empty; when virtually all active female religious orders have been feminized and paganized; when too few bishops and priests preach, teach, or defend the whole faith; when millions of teenagers fornicate; when we have almost ten million single-parent families, thanks to early fornication, then adultery, then easy divorce; when the typical U.S. family has fewer than two children; when about one-third of all married couples have been sterilized; when VD is out of control; when 100,000 have died from AIDS, and millions may be infected; when euthanasia is spreading fast; and when we're suffering from wars, crime, and natural disasters?

What other punishments God will inflict upon a nation that flings back into His face the gift of life, I don't know. I only know that it's high time for all of us to repent, pray, fast, and work as never before!

H.L.I. VISITS PUERTO RICO, U.S.A.

Father Matthew Habiger accompanied me on a mission journey to the "Enchanted Island" of Puerto Rico, February 4-11. Puerto Rico, which means "rich gate," is a tiny dot in the ocean beyond Cuba and Santo Domingo, four hours by air from Washington, DC.

Father Matthew claims he heard me give talks to bishops, seminarians, priests, nuns, young people, doctors, lawyers, news media people, married couples, marriage-encounter couples, singles, a university faculty, and others. He gave talks to many, too. It was surely one of the busiest HLI mission weeks ever, planned by Cuban Father Aurelio Adan, an organizational genius.

Father Adan runs Casa Manresa, a large study and retreat center high above the city of Aibonita, in the diocese of Caguas. In Caguas I taped a one-hour TV talk show, made three TV appearances, held several news conferences, addressed the priests of the diocese with Bishop Enrique Rodriguez translating, spoke at two of Puerto Rico's five major seminaries, and talked for one hour to the faculty of the Catholic University of Puerto Rico—my remarks being broadcast on TV and videotaped.

In 1493, on his second historic voyage, Christopher Columbus discovered the lush island, its rain forest, and its native Caribs. Eventually Spain took over. The Spaniards surrendered Puerto Rico to the USA in 1898; today the island is a commonwealth under the sovereignty of the U.S. senate. Puerto Ricans elect their own legislature and governor but can't vote for our president. This makes them, as they say, "last among equals."

Puerto Ricans hesitate to be classed as *norte-americanos*. Because of their "differentness," they've petitioned for dual citizenship, but the USA has already rejected that possibility. About half of the people prefer statehood, but it's a sensitive subject. Actually, the choices are statehood, independence, or enhanced commonwealth status. On 27 February 1991 a senate panel derailed and perhaps killed a bill to authorize a referendum for this year. The next possible time for a referendum is 1993. By the way, 2,500 Puerto Ricans fought for the USA coalition in the Gulf War.

Puerto Rico is a beautiful, mountainous, rectangular island, 100 miles long and 35 miles wide, filled with cars and traffic jams. It has 3.6 million people at home and 2 million abroad, mostly in the USA.

This small, green *Isla Encantada* supports four medical schools and three Catholic universities: the Catholic University of Puerto Rico at Ponce, Sacred Heart University in San Juan, and small Central University, run by the Dominicans, near San Juan. Some 30 percent of all students attend Catholic schools. Illiteracy is virtually unknown. Most Puerto Ricans are bilingual.

With people moving to and from the USA, statistics are hard to come by, but the average number of children per family is between two and three. The birthrate is definitely at replacement level with 1,000 more babies born in each of the last five years.

Almost overnight the island turned from an assortment of small farms and little villages to a highly industrialized society. The U.S. welfare system ruined farming. Some 25 percent of all Puerto Ricans are unemployed. The per-capita income is just $6,000, about 60 percent of the people being on food stamps (*versus* 8 percent on the mainland). Puerto Rico imports 90 percent of its food. A million tourists come to the island every year. Casinos were introduced recently for both *turistas* and Puerto Ricans. The chief exports are pharmaceuticals, small medical and electrical instruments, coffee, bananas, mangos, and pineapples.

The chief employers are U.S. companies, particularly pharmaceutical and electronics manufacturers lured by tax breaks, cheap labor, and the skills of the Puerto Ricans. Syntex and Searle produce their abortifacient pills here; Johnson & Johnson makes condoms. U.S. companies account for about half of the $22 billion in private investment on the island. Construction is the second-largest business, with tourism third. Puerto Rico enjoys an abundance of doctors and dentists.

A.I.D.S., ABORTION, P.P.

Because of promiscuity and drug abuse, AIDS is a huge problem. Some fifty babies have been diagnosed as HIV-positive. Last year, 400 Puerto Ricans died of AIDS; since 1987, the disease has killed 3,111. The virus has been found in 4,567 females and 5,678 males.

The AIDS plague is fast becoming heterosexual, thanks again to promiscuity (even among married people). An estimated 75 percent of all teens are promiscuous, many from their early teen years onward. Many mothers don't trust their daughters and take them to unscrupulous doctors who freely dispense the Pill to facilitate fornication.

There are no official abortion statistics, but estimates range from 35,000 to 100,000 per year. The floodgates opened with *Roe v. Wade* in 1973. Today seventeen big abortion mills are known, and doctors and even midwives perform abortions in an estimated seventy offices. Here, as in other Latin American countries, midwives, nurses, and others may initiate the abortion process, which is then completed in hospitals.

No one we spoke with knew how many abortuaries Planned Parenthood (PP) runs. Ensconced in the health and education departments, PP dispenses condoms ("to prevent AIDS") and abortifacient Pills through public hospitals. I met only one priest who seemed to be aware of PP's deadly, secret activity.

U.S. scientists used Puerto Rican women as guinea pigs when testing the abortifacient Pill in the 1950s. When the Pill raised havoc with the women's health, *Planificación Familiar* (PP) quietly introduced massive "surgical contraception" (sterilization) in the late sixties; today, according to medical literature, perhaps 40 percent of all couples, mostly the wives, have been neutered.

Puerto Rican girls tend to marry early and, after

bearing two children, are sterilized almost routinely (some 90 percent), often at only 20-21 years of age. As elsewhere

U.S. scientists used Puerto Rican women as guinea pigs when testing the abortifacient Pill in the 1950s.

in Latin America, women in mid-labor are pressured to sign documents permitting their sterilization. I asked Catholic laypeople whether priests actively promote chastity and preach against contraception, sterilization or even abortion; apparently, very few do.

PROLIFERS RESIST DEPOPULATORS

Great priests such as the pioneering Father Adan had 3,000 young people marching against abortion as early as 1973, but the prolife movement is very spotty, as is NFP. The only prolife literature and audiovisual aids we found were those sent by HLI's Latin American office in Miami over the last three years; we brought along a small mountain of new material.

There are several budding prolife groups, including an ecumenical one called Right to Life of Puerto Rico, which counts about 400 members and publishes a newsletter. They've picketed and rescued since 1986 and have closed a few abortuaries. The great bishop of Ponce, the Most Rev. Juan Fremio Torres, and his auxiliary, the Most Rev. Ricardo Surinach, have picketed and, reportedly, have rescued; they've been very encouraging to HLI.

Another small group (thirty-five members), known as the Movement for the Dignity of Life, is led by Luis Perez. Strangely, it works to enact a Living Will to prevent (!) euthanasia. I don't know whether I succeeded in persuading Señor Perez to drop his group's promotion of the Living Will as unnecessary and actually dangerous.

We've already agreed to sponsor an island-wide seminar at Casa Manresa next February to unite all the little prolife units. Then we'll spend three days in San Juan, the capital, doing radio and TV programs and addressing the many Catholic students. The gracious

Cardinal Luis Aponte-Martinez has invited us to supply films for the archdiocese's TV channel and audio cassettes for its two radio stations, and to speak to high-school and university students.

The island is 75 percent Catholic, with the Pentecostals claiming about 22 percent of the people and 5,000 churches. The militant Protestant sects have much money to work with. They quickly splinter and then get tax exemption for every church; in one city of 18,000 souls there are 100 such splinter churches. Members are asked to tithe 10 percent. We met Pentecostals begging money on the streets to set up more churches. They're very anti-Catholic: they've even interfered with Masses and weddings in the cathedral in Caguas by making loud noises outside.

Many uneducated Catholics fall for Pentecostal fanaticism, but I was told repeatedly that on their deathbeds they call for a priest. There's a persistent rumor (unconfirmed) that the abortion-pushing Rockefeller Foundation gave the sects $3 million to start more churches and neutralize the Catholic Church. Next to Guatemala, Puerto Rico is the most Protestantized Latin American country.

HOW HEALTHY A CHURCH?

There are four dioceses plus the Archdiocese of San Juan, headed by Cardinal Aponte-Martinez. He received us graciously and encouraged us, despite not feeling well. Each diocese runs a small major seminary. Only one actually completes the candidates' education for the priesthood; the other seminarians must go to Spain, Rome, or the mainland. There are a few small minor seminaries. Vocations are on the increase.

The island has 900 priests, of whom 60 percent are foreigners. There are many permanent deacons. The Archdiocese of San Juan alone claims 250 deacons in its 146 parishes. Parishes are huge, some numbering 50,000 souls. In Caguas, the cathedral and its neighboring chapels offer seventeen Masses every Sunday. The parish runs a grade school/high school for 2,500 students (tuition is $1,400). I brought the prolife message to 1,100 parishoners at a Sunday Mass attended by many professionals and their families. This parish exposes its many newlyweds to NFP, which seems little taught elsewhere.

The Redemptorists, followed by the Vincentians and the Jesuits, were modern Puerto Rico's pioneer religious group, coming in 1902 as the Spanish priests left. The Redemptorists have 65 members, a novitiate and philosophate in Puerto Rico, and a theologate in neighboring Santo Domingo. We Johnny-come-lately Benedictines have two monasteries, San Benito and San Antonio. Both run high schools said to be among the best on the island. There are more than twice as many nuns as priests, with many small religious communities.

Weekly Mass attendance is 10-20 percent, depending on the area. Priests and religious are too few; young Catholics learn their faith too little. The ubiquitous *Yanqui* culture and mass media bring in pornography on four TV

Priests and religious are too few; young Catholics learn their faith too little.

---

channels, on videocassettes, in theaters, and in the press.

Sister Petra of the Sisters of Mary of Schönstatt carries on a magnificent and varied apostolate in the classroom and the slums. Asked whether much theological confusion existed, the perceptive nun joked that there was "little theology on the island." "In Puerto Rico," she added, "the hellish message of Satan is packaged so beautifully, whereas the Church's message limps and too often doesn't get through." But 250 priests come to Father Adan's Casa Manresa for retreats yearly. So do many other religious, plus hosts of lay people, encounter groups, youth, and other apostolic souls who take their faith seriously and are wonderfully trained and nourished by Manresa's marvelous program.

PROLIFE NEWS MEDIA?!

Astonishingly, the media are more or less prolife, even though they give PP free advertising. While on a lecture tour of Taiwan in 1974, I was given fifteen minutes on national television and allowed to show any abortion photos I wanted to; rarely since then have I been able to do that, except in Puerto Rico.

Channel 4 in San Juan broadcast our posters of aborted babies and our fetal models. The producer told us he has never observed the fifteen studio personnel as attentive as they were during our ten-minute broadcast. They all seemed totally prolife, gratefully accepting the literature and badges we offered.

The soul of the Puerto Rican is still Catholic, but the Church suffers much because of too-few priests and religious and the hedonistic culture imported from the mainland. In spite of everything, the friendly Puerto Ricans remain family-oriented in the Latin American way.

It won't be hard to organize an authentic prolife thrust in Puerto Rico. Before next February's seminar, we'll pump in the best prolife/profamily literature and audiovisual aids in both Spanish and English. Our films and videos will be shown on TV and used widely. The bishops are deeply grateful for our friends' generosity to them through HLI.

We left more than $4,000 worth of the most effective films and videos in Puerto Rico; these will wake up thousands of people, save thousands of babies and expose PP's lies.

Another Island Starts to Sink

No. 80   May 1991

O ur tenth world Conference on love, life, and the family in Santa Clara, April 3-7, was a super-success! The gathering, with its simultaneous Spanish-language meeting and youth day, drew more than 2,000 people—twice as many as last year—from forty-seven countries. Our benefactors' prayers and those of nearby Our Lady of Peace parish, with its outstanding pastor, Father John Sweeny, made the conference a magnificent, unforgettable experience for all.

Gracing the meeting were four bishops from four countries, one abbot, fifty-six priests, thirteen nuns, several brothers and deacons, twenty seminarians and many other leaders. Many participants vowed to be with us in Ottawa for the eleventh world conference, April 29-May 3, 1992. *Special Report No. 81* will give you an overall summary of Santa Clara.

MAINE — A PROLIFE DESERT

Still exhausted from five intense days in Santa Clara and from consulting with so many wonderful people there, the following weekend I headed for Portland, Maine—which Planned Parenthood (PP) had just moved into. Before this, I had spoken on prolife themes at least once in every one of our fifty states except Wyoming and Maine (where I had, however, made several mission appeals years ago). The prolife situation in Maine, which has one million people and one diocese of 250,000 Catholics, was the worst I've seen yet.

Benedictine Bishop Joseph J. Gerry of Portland is

Benedictinitis is a too-common disease that prevents you from facing thorny problems.

---

adept at noninvolvement in prolife. He seems to suffer from Benedictinitis, a too-common disease that prevents you from facing thorny problems (thus, you don't need to do anything about them). Despite repeated attempts, prolife leaders can't get to their bishop.

Bishop Gerry, former abbot of New Hampshire's St. Anselm's Abbey, occasionally writes vaguely about the right to life. But typically, he's incapable of supporting or generating needed action, or unwilling to do so. Where is the Church's prolife pastoral program in Maine, after twenty-eight million unborn babies have been killed?

Many prolifers were disappointed by the diocese's refusal to oppose a recent "gay rights" bill. Diocesan officials refused to testify; they wasted a priceless opportunity to educate the public about the disastrous results of such laws, already evident in other cities and states. For example, two women in Madison, Wisconsin, advertised for a roommate to share apartment expenses but refused to accept lesbians. Under a "gay rights" ordinance, they were fined $1,500 and forced to attend a "sensitivity training" class taught by homosexuals.

Another example: in St. Paul, Minnesota, a homosexual applied for a job as an eighth-grade music teacher at a Catholic school. On religious grounds, the school refused to hire him. He sued under the city's "gay rights" law, and the local human-rights commission found the Church guilty of discrimination.

Thank God, Maine's homosexual bill was defeated for now, despite the lobbying of a Catholic pastor and columnist, Father Roger P. Chabot.

WHERE IS THE CHURCH?

Earlier, Maine had passed a Living Will bill. Typically, some legislators now want to make three dangerous changes amounting to creeping euthanasia. Alert prolife laypeople are fighting back; Church officials are doing nothing.

Not one priest or pastor has surfaced to support Maine's prolifers. The state's right-to-life convention draws only 150 people. Pope-bashing Father Richard McBrien, the rebel theologian who heads Notre Dame's theology department, airs his strange column in *Church World*, Maine's insipid Catholic weekly. (Loyal Catholics rejoiced that Father Andrew Greeley withdrew *his* column.) Girl "altar boys" abound.

Mercy Hospital, run by the Mercy sisters and purportedly Catholic, joined the University of Southern Maine and four other groups in sponsoring an obviously New Age "Healthy Day for Kids" to foster "self-esteem and empowerment," with plenty of pop psychology, occultism, foods from "the Earth," "a peace educator," "massage for kids," "Kid-Power Shields," "clowning and dancing"—but not a trace of Christian morality or idealism.

The advertising asked, "Why should you send your children to Healthy Day for Kids?" The answer: "Easy ways to take care of their minds, bodies, and inner selves [in terms of what?]; why it feels good to make healthy choices [choices in terms of what?]; how growing inside is as important as growing outside [how and with what?]." Alas, the New Age religion, "values clarification" (read: nullification), and a subtle, dressed-up, but thinly disguised humanism have taken deep root. Please pray for Maine.

IRELAND: SAFE HAVEN NO MORE

Good Catholic parents often ask me whether there are any havens left in the world to which they can escape to raise their children. The answer is always no. Theological rebellion and confusion, weak bishops (there are exceptions, of course), the collapse of the Catholic school system, immoral sex "education," condom/AIDS programs in schools, empty seminaries and novitiates, family-destroying feminism, pagan mass media, AIDS, women's religious communities' embracing of feminism and often a false pacifism, etc., etc., are universal phenomena in the Western world, or in those countries that have a Western culture, such as Australia and New Zealand.

Not even Ireland is solid any more. In 1972 I met with Dublin's Archbishop Dermot Ryan to warn him of the coming abortion threat. I explained to him how the Irish Family Planning Association (IFPA), an affiliate of the infamous London-based International Planned Parenthood Federation (IPPF), had established itself in his country in 1969.

I explained to the politely listening Archbishop Ryan that IFPA was ignoring the Irish law banning the sale of contraceptives; that it was IPPF's declared international policy to break the law in order to change it; that I'd been in more than thirty countries and had seen that contraception, promoted by PP, always led to legalized abortion; and that there wasn't a single country anywhere that had avoided legalizing abortion after allowing widespread contraception and the fornication and other sexual sins that contraception engenders.

I offered him documentation from IFPA/IPPF. To my astonishment, he gently refused to accept it. He told me it was ridiculous to think that the Irish would ever be faced with legalizing abortion, because, "after all, Ireland is a totally Catholic country. Contraception, maybe; abortion, never." My final remark was that, since England had legalized abortion-on-demand just across the Irish Sea in April 1967, surely Ireland would be faced with it sooner or later. The gracious archbishop gently ushered me to the door. "Your Grace," I thought, "you will see the day!"

THE CRACK IN THE DAM

And Archbishop Ryan did see the day. Six years later, with diabolical propaganda, the first permissive contraception law appeared. The Health (Family Planning) Act was first introduced in December 1978. It passed in 1979 and became law by the introduction of the regulations on 1 November 1980. Sadly, the bishops didn't oppose this nation-destroying legislation.

It was a complicated bill that allowed non-medical contraceptives (not abortifacients) to be distributed only by sales from pharmacists for *bona fide* "family planning." It allowed "clinics" such as the IFPA to give advice on contraceptives but not to supply them. Contraceptives were to be issued only by a doctor's prescription and only to married couples. In many ways, the bill was a sham that couldn't be enforced. The IFPA was the first to break it by selling contraceptives; it was not prosecuted.

In February 1985 a "liberalizing" bill passed on a close vote. It made "non-medical contraceptives" available to anyone over the age of eighteen through licensed pharmacies, clinics, and medical practitioners. Archbishop Ryan's successor, Archbishop Kevin McNamara, was the only bishop to oppose it. The minister of health was Barry Desmond of the Labor Party; as it turned out, he was a member of the IFPA. (True to the Gospel, the children of this world, and especially PP, often work harder than the children of light—especially when there's no episcopal awareness or leadership.)

Of course, anyone who knew PP and its methods knew that PP wouldn't stop at "limited" contraception. But did the bishops and priests and professors know? Of course not; but if *I* knew, why didn't they? Today contraception

---

> *Of course, anyone who knew PP and its*
> *methods knew that PP wouldn't stop at*
> *"limited" contraception.*

---

and abortifacients are available to anyone eighteen or older, married or single, and the propaganda for contraception/sterilization/abortion moves on with relentless inevitability. The latest suggestion: contraceptives for anyone sixteen years old or older, supposedly to prevent AIDS and VD. Prime Minister Charles Haughey is pushing this proposal.

PROLIFE YANKS WARN IRELAND

Should I have believed Archbishop Ryan and abandoned the Irish? No, in conscience I could not. I don't know how many talks I gave in all parts of Ireland to all kinds of groups during several mission journeys, how many slide shows I did, or how many films I fed into that country. I warned the Irish that because they had a U.S.-style constitution (approved in 1937) they were likely to find their five-member Supreme Court giving them what we got, a decision imposing abortion-on-demand.

Some Catholic high schools, such as that of the Christian Brothers in Cork, refused to allow me to "contaminate their boys." The anti-Catholic, pro-abortion media deceitfully misreported what I said and crucified me for "shocking" young people with models of unborn babies.

The youth, as they do everywhere, responded favorably to me—except for some university students, especially at the prestigious, anti-Catholic Trinity College Dublin.

A few dissident theologians, such as the still-teaching Father Enda McDonagh, tried to prevent me from addressing seminarians and university students at Ireland's national St. Patrick's Seminary at Maynooth. Finally, thanks to pressure from alert laymen and the rector, the theologians were overruled by the future archbishop, Father/Dr. Kevin McNamara.

I spoke to 700 seminarians and students; six seminarians fainted, or pretended to (I still don't know which), when I showed them the film "Abortion—A Woman's Decision." I recall the farsighted future archbishop's telling me, at a little party afterward, that when pictures of aborted babies no longer cause some people to faint, we must really start worrying.

HLI's forerunner, the Human Life Center (then headquartered at St. John's University in Minnesota), which I founded in 1972 after much opposition, spent some $100,000 to save Irish babies from legalized abortion. A crucial weekend conference of some fifty carefully chosen Irish prolife leaders and three Americans—Dr. Herbert Ratner, Carl Anderson, and yours truly—was particularly effective.

The conference, financed by the DeRance Foundation, took place in a convent on the outskirts of Dublin. With only one Irish priest present, the savvy Father R. Neville, we laid plans to save the Green Isle from the worst. Our conclusion: the only way the Irish could save themselves from the death peddlers' onslaught was to pass a constitutional amendment which, in effect, affirmed that Irish babies were protected from conception onward.

On 7 September 1983 the national referendum took place; the prolifers won with 63.5 percent of the vote. No future government can enact an abortion law without first going to the people with a referendum.

Incidentally, once awakened to the abortion menace, Archbishop Ryan performed splendidly; later, as head of the Pontifical Congregation for the Propagation of the Faith, he thanked me profusely. Today Ireland is the only

European country that doesn't legally kill her preborn babies—except, of course, through the Pill and IUD.

MORAL DECAY & A SHRINKING BIRTHRATE

But what has happened to Ireland since the early eighties? No man is an island, and no nation is, either—even if it's surrounded by water. Ireland is too close to the corruption of England. The UK's pagan mass media, including the BBC, bring the worst of modern hedonism to the "Land of Saints and Scholars." On 28 July 1986, the Irish defeated divorce in a referendum by a margin of 67.6 percent, despite ferocious propaganda from the anti-Catholic media.

When the European Economic Community (EEC) began proceedings to force Ireland to conform to other European countries by killing preborn babies, the Irish made it clear that they'd rather leave the organization than comply, despite the fearsome economic consequences for Ireland.

Not all is well in Ireland. Many young people leave because of the unemployment rate of almost 20 percent. Ireland has a high foreign debt, almost $23 billion. Materially, only Portugal is poorer in Western Europe; but spiritually, Ireland is the richest. Still, the bishops' national magazine, *Inter-Com*, and the top religious journals, *The Forum* and *Doctrine and Life*, show that New Age thinking is rife and that Ireland is in definite moral decline.

Nationally, Sunday Mass attendance has fallen to 70 percent—still the highest in Europe, by far. Increasingly, the Irish are practicing contraception, and sterilization—the fastest-growing means of birth "control" in the world—is taking its toll also. The bishops have promoted natural family planning (NFP) feebly. There are, however, two independent national lay NFP organizations, which I've addressed twice. The bishops' national organization, called the Catholic Marriage Advisory Council, provides only a nominal NFP service; it's not committed to orthodoxy.

The birthrate has fallen to 2.1 children per family; it's

still the highest in the EEC, where the average family includes only 1.58 children (the world average is 3.4). But Ireland is the only EEC country with an annual *emigration* of nearly 12.5 people per 1,000. This outflow offsets the birthrate of 14.7 per 1,000 (in 1980 it was 21.9). The emigrants are usually young people, who bear their children elsewhere. So their departure is a significant factor in Ireland's declining rates of marriages and births.

Even so, Ireland is a young country, 30 percent of her people being under thirty years of age, with a slight increase in births currently. Because surgical abortions are totally forbidden, Ireland boasts the healthiest women in a

---

Because surgical abortions are totally forbidden, Ireland boasts the healthiest women in a dying Europe.

---

dying Europe—a clear refutation of the universal feminist lie that women need legal abortion for their health. Irish women aren't dying through back-alley abortions, either.

Seminaries and novitiates are becoming emptier and emptier. No longer is Ireland a source of missionary vocations. Poland is now the only Western country producing a good number of priests and nuns for the mission world. Last year the Poles ordained 1,100 priests (!); 200 priests and nuns entered foreign missions.

Meanwhile, each year the English lure some 4,000 Irish colleens to England to have their babies killed, even though the Irish courts have forbidden feminist groups and PP to refer or usher girls to Britain for that purpose. Out-of-wedlock births increased 80 percent between 1984 and 1989, and almost doubled in the year 1989-90.

CONDOM-PEDDLING & THEOBABBLE

As in other lands, Irish university students more and more want to have sterile fornication, again reflecting a gradual moral breakdown. Student unions are more than tinged with Marxism. For students and other young people, IFPA chose Valentine's Day, 1988, to open an illegal condom-peddling stall in the Virgin record store in Dublin's center. The Green Isle, however, has registered comparatively few AIDS cases, the lowest rate in Europe (Switzerland reports the highest); these cases are due mostly to increasing drug use. The government says there are about 1,720 Irish citizens with HIV.

Typically, the *New York Times* (1 January 1991) smeared the Church as a great obstacle to AIDS prevention in Ireland because of her stand against the government's compulsory AIDS-"education" program in public secondary schools and against the government's financing of drug treatment centers in Dublin that offer condoms, clean needles and counseling. As happens everywhere else, condom/AIDS/sex "education" will only increase sexual immorality. As it does everywhere, IFPA uses the AIDS scare to plead for universal distribution of condoms.

According to 1989 World Health Organization (WHO) figures, there were 1.3 diagnosed cases of AIDS in Ireland for every 100,000 people, *versus* 13.3 in the USA. Although there are efforts to legalize sodomy, homosexuality isn't a big problem yet, and so only 135 homosexual men are infected with the virus. So far, 69 babies are known to have been born with AIDS. Both the government's and the Church's AIDS-"education" programs are highly controversial.

The bishops published a defense of *Humanae Vitae*, but they weren't exactly enthusiastic about that encyclical. They tolerated a few wild, Curran/McCormick/McBrien-like theologians, such as Father Enda McDonagh, who, with a few others, has fouled up theology at the various seminaries.

When Father James Goode, a lecturer on medical ethics at University College Cork, dissented from *Humanae Vitae*, then-Bishop Cornelius Lucey removed him from office immediately—the kind of thing U.S. bishops didn't do, and still don't. Today we're paying an enormous price for this negligence. But most of the harm in Ireland was done by priests' generally ignoring *Humanae Vitae* or undermining it through "pastoral applications."

PRESIDENT ROBINSON'S BRAVE NEW IRELAND

One sign of a changing Ireland was last year's election of the lawyer Mary Robinson as the country's president, with

---

One sign of a changing Ireland was last year's election of the lawyer Mary Robinson as the country's president.

---

the help of the viciously anti-Catholic media. Her dream, and that of the bishop-lampooning media, is to produce a brave, new "pluralistic" Ireland; she was a loud and eloquent opponent of ours in our campaign to prevent the legalization of abortion in the 1980s.

Facing only a milk-toast opponent, the ultra-feminist Robinson lied again and again during the campaign, e.g., by denying she supported abortion; the truth is, she favors abortion, contraception, divorce, sterilization, homosexuality, and a few more evils. Naturally, Eleanor Smeal, the ex-Catholic, pro-abort president of the USA's Feminist Majority, honored the new president of Ireland.

Most of the people weren't aware of Robinson's deadly agenda. She got into office through an electoral fluke I've no room to explain here—but even so, her election tells us much about modern, changing Ireland. So does the recent passage of a marital rape law to please the feminists; it will only increase the number of abortion promoting/ referring rape-crisis centers run by angry, pro-abort feminists.

WILL ARCHBISHOP DALY ACT?

Long before he became bishop of Down and Connor (Belfast) in northern Ireland and, last December 16, the archbishop of Armagh and therefore primate of all Ireland, Cahal Daly wrote an excellent book, *Morals, Law, and Life*. In this magnificent refutation of the ideas of an agnostic British legal scholar, Glanville Williams, he intelligently defended the Church's teachings on the evils of contraception, sterilization, abortion, and euthanasia.

But as a bishop, and even when he was head of Catholic education, the popular Daly has been a disappointment. For example, he's an outspoken enemy of the Irish Republican Army (IRA) but a good friend of the occupying British government. In 1795 the British decided to build the national seminary at Maynooth; they wanted priests and bishops who would keep their flocks from rebelling against British oppression.

The 73-year-old Bishop Daly once compared the IRA to the "Al Capone gangsterism of Chicago." But he has encouraged Catholics to join the Royal Ulster Constabulary (RUC), which tortures nationalist prisoners, ransacks Catholic families' homes, kills children by means of plastic bullets, and is accused of aiding pro-British death squads that murder his people. He also urges Catholics to join the British Army's brutal Ulster Defence Regiment (UDR). Lately, however, he has made some remarks slightly favorable to nationalism. We were never able to involve him in the anti-abortion fight.

The ecumenically experienced Bishop Daly will have his hands full wrestling with Ireland's inter-Church situation. Example: in early 1990, strangely, the Church of Ireland became the first Anglican Church in Europe to approve the ordination of priestesses and women bishops. Within a year, four women were ordained. Typically, three senior Catholic clergy, including the abbot of Glenstal, Aidan Shea, OSB, attended the first woman's ordination in Dublin!

Another example: last year the large Irish Presbyterian Church in northern Ireland, led by the infamous anti-Catholic bigot, Rev. Ian Paisley, would have no part of the newly formed British and Irish Council of Churches because Britain's Catholic Church was a member.

According to the *Irish Times* (28 December 90):

There are 15,634 religious in Ireland, of whom 73 percent are nuns, 19 percent priests, and 8 percent brothers. There are 11,415 nuns spread over 152 orders, 3,041 priests spread over 44 orders and 1,178 brothers from 11 congregations. Over the past twenty years, religious orders have declined far more than the secular clergy. Only 2 percent of nuns are under 30, 70 percent are over 50, and 12 percent are over 80; 5 percent of the brothers are under 30, 69 percent over 50, and 6 percent over 80; 9 percent of the priests are under 30, 68 percent over 50 and 10 percent over 80.

How sad it is that the great, weather-beaten, old Irish missionaries—nuns and priests I met in Africa—won't be replaced because of the birth/vocation dearth in the West. On the other hand, they did their work so well that native Africans are now able to take over.

Please pray for Ireland to Our Lady of Knock.

Fr. Marx with Malaysian nuns dedicated to nurturing souls in the Kingdom of God.

Archbishop Frantisek Vanak of Olomouc, Czechoslovakia, and Fr. Marx.

A Conference for the Millennium

No. 81   June 1991

Father **Matthew Habiger** and I are still in a state of semi-trauma after becoming the first Western prolife/profamily leaders to visit the USSR. In Vilnius, capital of Soviet-occupied Lithuania, we did a three-day seminar. More than 400 people attended, including many doctors and state health officials. At our seminar in Katowice, Poland, we attracted more than 500, including many doctors and church leaders. The third seminar took place in Bratislava, Slovakia, where 1,400 crowded in; 200-300 others were turned away! I'm overflowing with inside information (both good news and bad); most of it will have to wait for future *Special Reports*. But here's a glimpse:

HORROR STORIES FROM THE RED ARMY

The more you learn about the liberated countries behind the fallen curtain, the more hideous the face of Communism appears. At our Dresden conference last fall, I spoke to East Germans who'd had a chance to see the living quarters of the occupying Soviet soldiers. "Indescribable," they recalled. "Worse than a pigsty." And yet these soldiers didn't want to go home, so bad are the living conditions in the USSR.

Enforcing armed-service duty has resulted in death and crippling from beatings, whippings, and shootings. Brutal officers reportedly inflict unbelievable tortures; an autopsy on one victim, nineteen-year-old Vitaly Levina, revealed he'd been beaten, stabbed, and raped. Deserting soldiers come home to their mothers with bleeding and festering wounds, not knowing where to go or where to hide.

In the last four years, 15,000 Soviet soldiers have died while in military service—ten per day. Just about as many perished in nine years of war in Afghanistan. One out of every five of the 15,000 committed suicide. Many die in too-realistic training exercises.

Soldiers' mothers threatened to throw themselves under rolling tanks during Moscow's October Revolution celebrations if nothing were done about the horrid situation. When they confronted Gorbachev with pictures of their tortured or dead sons, he admitted, "It doesn't look good for our army," and promised to appoint a commission to study the situation.

But the National Committee of Soldiers' Mothers wants more: recognition of the right of conscientious objection, reform of living conditions in the armed services, minimal health care, placement of mothers on draft boards, and access to barracks and hospitals for inspection. Only healthy young men should be conscripted, they insist, and no soldier should be made a part of, or blamed for, internal conflicts. (The USSR is a prison-house of dozens of nationalities, cultures, and religions.)

THE FRUITS OF ATHEISM

The ancient saying, *homo hominis lupus*—"man is a wolf to man"—fits life in a land where God was officially and systematically outlawed for eighty years. In such a godless society, humans soon begin to live like animals. And, as the great Russian writer Feodor Dostoyevsky wrote, "If God is not, nothing is morally wrong."

We've learned something of the horrifying state of the Soviet public-health system. For example, no anesthesia is given, usually, to the six to ten million women who abort their babies each year (there are about five million births). The mothers' shrieks of pain are often met with insults from the medical staff, even though 75 percent of all Soviet doctors are women.

One report on Soviet medical practice begins, "SOS! We don't want to die," and concludes with the chilling words, "All we can do is wait for death to deliver us." At our Dresden meeting, an expatriate Soviet doctor described how medics and medicine were used to torture prisoners. Medical experiments on human beings were common.

And now the mothers face another worry: pornography, totally out of control because anti-porn laws aren't being enforced. There are filthy magazines, sex manuals, and long queues outside of the 25,000 video salons specializing in foreign movies filled with sex and violence. All of these will lead to more rapes, "date rapes," rape-murders, child molestations, mental illness, suicides, divorces, VD, and AIDS.

Recently the national legislature, the Supreme Soviet, easily passed a resolution to set up a panel to draw the fine line "between harmless erotica and nasty pornography" (*Los Angeles Times*, 13 April 91). But surely this panel won't stem the growing public outcry against the porn films. Girlie calendars and sex manuals are flooding a disorganized, disoriented, disillusioned "evil empire" at unprecedented levels. Russian nationalist writer Valentin Rasputin has warned of a "spiritual Chernobyl" threatening the USSR.

Meanwhile, 17,000 East German women and children have been abandoned by husbands seeking new fortunes (and new mates) in West Germany.

WORLD CONFERENCE DOUBLES IN SIZE; VATICAN REP ATTENDS

Every year I pick a hotel that I think will be big enough for our world conference, and this year I thought I'd been especially smart. I selected a Marriott hotel in Santa Clara with two separate towers to house us and five large

---

Father Paul Marx: "This year," I thought, "no sardine syndrome!"

---

meeting rooms that we could fill simultaneously; I put the entire Hispanic section across the street in a separate hotel, with its own meeting rooms, exhibit area, and so on. "This year," I thought, "no sardine syndrome!"

I guess the Lord decided to teach me another lesson in humility, because our tenth world conference was absolutely bursting at the seams—the biggest ever. Nine hundred more people were on hand this year, an increase we could never have predicted. Total registration was almost 2,000 (not counting Youth Day). Besides Masses, homilies, rosaries, processions, banquets, and special meetings, the conference held 68 regular sessions, taught by an international faculty—the top prolife experts in the world, bar none.

And this year the Vatican was watching us as never before. An official Vatican representative, Monsignor Francisco Gil Hellin, was sent to attend the entire event, bringing official messages of greeting and commendation from the Holy Father and from Cardinal Alfonso Lopez Trujillo, head of the Pontifical Council for the Family.

A clue to explain the Holy See's heightened interest in our conference may have been given by Father Malachi Martin in a provocative and wide-ranging address at our Saturday banquet, a real highlight of the conference. I'll come back to this matter later.

TRUTH SQUAD UNMASKS RU-486 HOAX

First, let me stress an aspect of our conferences that's always important but was especially prominent this year: the truth-squad aspect. All year long, the propagandists for abortion, antilife technologies, sex "education," and population control have free rein in the media. They're hardly ever answered. But at our conferences they're not only answered but exposed for all the world to see. Our faculty acts as a truth squad.

For example, Planned Parenthood (PP) and its allies have been saying for the last year or so that RU-486 isn't just an abortion pill. They say it has other, legitimate uses: to treat breast cancer, meningeoma (brain tumor), Cushing's disease (a pituitary and adrenal disorder), various other cancers, and maybe even AIDS. I've been perplexed myself over how we could keep RU-486 out of the country when these other uses were cropping up.

Enter Dr. Bernard Nathanson. He addressed us on Saturday morning, and his talk was a revelation. It seems that all these claims of RU-486's benefits have but a single scholarly source—an article in the *Journal of the American Medical Association* (August 1990) by a Dr. William Regelson. The *JAMA* article carried footnote references to the scientific studies on which the claims are supposedly based. Thus, Regelson's footnotes have become the one and only way that doubters could check up on these alleged benefits.

Thank God that Dr. Nathanson was a doubter. He followed up each footnote, tracking down the often obscure journals in which the original research appeared and reading it for himself. The result? Every one of Regelson's claims was a "shameless scam," unsupported by the doctor's own footnotes! According to Regelson's own sources:

—RU-486 did *not* cure breast cancer, had no effect on its metastases, and didn't help a single patient to live longer;

—the study on meningeomas never even mentions RU-486 but reports that results with similar drugs were "inconclusive to disappointing";

—the experiment on using RU-486 for Cushing's disease was never followed up by anyone, because the original trial was too unpromising, as its authors themselves admit;

—no evidence supports any claimed benefit in the treatment of any kind of cancer whatever, and one of the papers Regelson "cited" doesn't even exist; and

—not a single scientific paper in world medical literature suggests that RU-486 can help with AIDS in any way.

(A week after this talk, Dr. Jerome Lejeune, the famed French geneticist, told me in Bratislava, "RU-486 has only one capability, to kill unborn babies.")

After sharing his intellectual detective work with us, Dr. Nathanson exposed the motive for PP's campaign of deceit: the abortionists hope to get the FDA to approve RU-486 for a non-abortion-related purpose so that prolife forces won't fight it, believing the FDA isn't considering approval of the drug for abortion purposes. But here's the trick: once the FDA approves a drug for *any* use, it cannot disapprove it for any *other* use. The agency has no power to ban any use of a drug, once it has let that drug enter the country. Did you know that? I'll bet not one prolifer in a hundred did.

RAIN FORESTS & OZONE HOLES

Here's another example of the truth-squad function of our faculty: You've heard about the greenhouse effect, the disappearance of the world's rain forests, and the hole in the ozone layer. You've heard that all these crises demand depopulation. Well, Dr. Jacqueline Kasun, who also spoke to us that Saturday morning, tore the mask off these "crises."

Take the situation in Brazil, so widely publicized. The forested area of Brazil today is so big you could fit the entire state of California into it *fourteen times*. The fraction that is cut down each year is just six-tenths of one percent.

Now, when you express this operation in square miles, it sounds large (and it is), but the scare-mongers never tell us that the 0.6 percent cut each year is less than the

---

The scare-mongers never tell us that the 0.6 percent cut each year is less than the volume of timber growth occurring each year.

---

volume of timber *growth* occurring each year. That's right, the amount cut is less than the amount of new growth. The bottom line: Brazil isn't much different from any other country in terms of forest stability. And listen to this: the world's total forested area (four billion hectares) is the same size today as it was in 1950.

Now take the greenhouse effect. (Please.) It's true that over the last 100 years, the proportion of carbon dioxide in the atmosphere has risen from around 280 parts per million to something more than 350 parts per million. It's also true that our cities have become hotter, because too many shade trees have been eliminated by streets, highways, parking lots, and so forth (the real deforestation is urban, not global).

But is there any evidence that *world temperatures* are rising? According to Dr. Kasun, neither the researchers at the National Oceanic and Atmospheric Agency (NOAA) nor the scientists at MIT have been able to find any upward trend. The oceans, for example, are just as cold today as they were in 1856!

Lastly, consider the ozone hole over the Antarctic (and now it is said that there may be one over the Arctic). Is it something to worry about? Maybe. But then, maybe not. No one really knows. Science could give a more definite answer if we had a credible theory of ozone formation in the first place. We're never told that the existing scientific models cannot account for fully *one-half* of the ozone in our earth's atmosphere right now!

Where can you get information like this, except from the truth squad we assemble every year? I wonder how many specialist publications and technical journals you'd have to subscribe to, and how many hours you'd have to spend reading them, just to get the vital facts that we received on one Saturday morning at our conference. Let me give you some more examples.

DANGER OF "GAY" PARENTS DOCUMENTED

Since 1970, more than forty articles in the social-science literature have dealt with the topic of homosexuals' acting as parents (adoptive or otherwise). Their authors all claim that the "sexual orientation" of the parents makes no difference in how the children turn out. This "evidence" is now being used in court battles all over the USA, to secure adoption rights and custody of minor children for avowed homosexuals.

But on Thursday morning, the first full day of our conference, Dr. Paul Cameron of the Family Research Institute gave us a sneak preview of new data which, when published later this year, will blow this myth out of the water. Dr. Cameron has made the first-ever random sampling of urban adults, investigating current "sexual orientation," relations with parents, and so on.

Out of more than 5,000 people, Dr. Cameron found a small fraction who had been raised by one or more homosexual parents. Only 2 to 3 percent of the sample population said they were bisexual or homosexual, but *35 percent* of those who had been raised by a homosexual said they were bisexual or homosexual today. In other words, children raised by deviates were *ten times* more likely to turn out abnormal than children raised by normal parents! I wish every judge who hears adoption and custody cases could be shown this powerful new evidence.

SEX ED: AN ATTACK ON TRUTH

Dr. William Coulson has served on our faculty before, and you may have heard his provocative talk "Confessions of a Catholic-School Dismantler." It concerns his role as a top expert in educational psychology in close collaboration with Carl Rogers and Abraham Maslow, whose theories he rejected when he saw that their implementation destroyed once-thriving Catholic institutions. (Rogers and Maslow themselves repudiated the theories eventually, although many Catholic school administrators still don't know it.)

Now Dr. Coulson is turning his formidable expertise to a new area of controversy, perhaps the hottest of all: he's offering a psychological evaluation of sex education.

We heard plenty of debate over sex "education" at Santa Clara, mostly over two topics: interpreting the various papal statements on the subject (Jim Likoudis and Father Marc Calegari debated), and airing the controversy between Randy Engel and Coleen Kelly Mast (the two women themselves debated, as well as Father Casimir Peterson and Father Calegari). Some people told me they were disconcerted by these sometimes-heated debates, but I thought they were healthful. Where there truly is room for disagreement among prolife/profamily activists, it's important that people realize that, listen to both sides, and prepare themselves to form a prudent judgment.

Still, I don't think our staged debates shed as much light on the issue as did this one particular talk (on Thursday afternoon) by Dr. Coulson.

Dr. Coulson attacked the "nondirective" methodology that's built into sex-ed programs (often covertly). For purposes of comparison, he took us through the Growing Healthy curriculum and the Quest program—two highly touted "drug education" programs. Both contain plenty of accurate information about the health hazards of smoking and the dangers of drug use.

But the atmosphere is one of discussion, using the "nondirective" model, in which the teacher becomes more of a "facilitator." The pros and cons are laid out, perhaps very well; but in the last analysis, it's up to the student to decide what his "values" are.

It's this basic atmosphere that makes these programs failures, Dr. Coulson pointed out. Objective followup studies show that kids who've been through these two programs are *more likely* to smoke and to try drugs than their peers who've had no drug "education" at all. In fact, he revealed, the R.J. Reynolds Tobacco Company knows that and is *paying* for the Quest program in Puerto Rico and elsewhere. It has found a form of "anti-smoking education" that actually increases the market for their product!

Now look at PP and the sex-ed programs they support. The programs have the same "nondirective" format, and Dr. Coulson suggests PP knows what R.J. Reynolds knows: any such program will increase sexual experimentation, teen pregnancy, and therefore the market for PP's "services," from condoms to abortions.

Psychologically speaking, whenever we tell children (explicitly or implicitly) that what we're trying to get across is "values," we're declining to transmit *truth*. We're becoming passive. We're letting the hucksters move in and play the *real* formative role in our children's lives.

When I heard this observation, I thought, "The truth squad strikes again! Now I'm learning the deep and subtle criterion by which to judge sex-'education' programs. Never mind how much orthodoxy they've had pumped into them as 'information' on the Church's teachings; the real test is whether they encourage 'nondirective' discussions in which, ultimately, the *student* is put in a position to 'decide.'"

SPIRITUAL TREASURES FROM THE MASTERS

Now let me show you some of the spiritual and theological

treasures offered at Santa Clara. Monsignor William Smith is, for my money, the finest moral theologian in the USA, and this year he treated us to three brilliant talks. They dealt with the nature and formation of conscience, the role of moral principles, and dissent from *Humanae Vitae.*

The three topics are closely connected, of course, because when people deny the role of absolute moral principles, they falsely exalt individual conscience to

---

When people deny the role of absolute moral principles, they falsely exalt individual conscience to "infallible" status.

"infallible" status and then use it to justify dissent and worse. But when you hear these topics explained by a real master, the Church's teaching becomes wonderfully clear and compelling. That was everyone's reaction; in fact, the tapes of Monsignor Smith's talks sold out so quickly that we couldn't keep them in stock.

Equally hot sellers were the tapes of Father John Hardon's. His talk on the state of catechetics was particularly impressive. As you know, catechetics is a disaster area (one religious community in Detroit recently closed thirty-one schools in a single year, and vocations to teaching orders have dropped 90 percent since 1965). The horrifying loss of faith behind these trends is reflected in the textbooks themselves.

Father Hardon took us through an examination of five errors that dominate the "updated" series: Nestorianism (making Christ merely a human person), Pelagianism (exalting human nature at the expense of the supernatural), conciliarism (making the "spirit" of Vatican II higher than papal authority), sexualism (portraying the Church's moral teachings as obstacles to permissible and praiseworthy pleasures), and laicism (abolishing the distinction between the ordained priesthood and the laity).

In the face of these errors, Father Hardon reported two promising developments. One is the universal catechism, now being prepared by a commission directed by Cardinal

Joseph Ratzinger. The other is a plan to establish an International Catechetical Institute for the Family. It will train parents to teach the faith to their own children—a marvelous way to bypass the heretical "middle management" that has corrupted Catholic education in so many dioceses.

Still another "best seller" was the magnificent Catholic philosopher, Dr. Alice von Hildebrand. She spoke on Edith Stein as a model of femininity, on the true philosophy of love (*eros* and *agape*), and on the roots of radical feminism in Simone de Beauvoir.

Philosophy is often dry and merely theoretical, but in Dr. von Hildebrand's hands it becomes an instrument of life-changing insight. She helps you glimpse the moral beauty of the truth, as Edith Stein came to discover it. And you see the soul-destroying character of the flight from the truth, personified by Jean-Paul Sartre and the radical feminists. I cannot recommend her talks highly enough.

H.L.I.'S ROLE IN THE GLOBAL SHOWDOWN

Now let me return to the topic of why the Vatican was so interested in our Conference.

Instead of looking at the worldwide conflict between prolife and antilife forces as a *moral* struggle (which, of course, it is, on one level), Father Malachi Martin invited us to look at it as a geopolitical calculation.

International PP serves as a convenient pawn of the state departments of the Western nations. A grand alliance of the birth-dearth countries is reaching out to the de-Communizing East, and it's moving to exclude the birth-rich global South by frantically pushing depopulation technologies on the southern hemisphere and other developing nations. That's the geopolitical reality of what's going on today, with the flow of Western development capital going into the East Bloc (or ex-Bloc), and the flow of Western pills, sterilants, and abortifacients pouring into the Third World.

Of course, the Western powers need a cover. Therefore, a nongovernmental organization such as PP is indispensable. It makes chemical warfare against developing populations seem like international humanitarian aid.

Why is the Vatican watching all this activity and watching HLI? Is it just because we're PP's worst enemy,

---

The Vatican believes this global struggle will come to a climax in the nine years that remain in this millennium.

---

worldwide? No, there's a further reason. The Vatican believes this global struggle will come to a climax in the nine years that remain in this millennium, and Pope John Paul II holds this belief on the strength of the Third Secret of Fatima.

In this geopolitical struggle the whole future of the human race is at stake, and wherever the cause of humanity is at stake, Father Martin observed, there the Woman is engaged. We were all at stake in Eden, and there she was promised to us as the one whose seed would crush the head of the serpent. We were all at stake on a Friday afternoon in Jerusalem, and there she was present at the foot of the Cross.

We are all at stake again in these closing years of the twentieth century, as this deadly battle between parenthood and sterility, between seed and anti-seed, comes to a deadly climax. If we don't win in this decade, mankind will be set on an irreversible course of population implosion. The Polish pope believes that Christ *will* intervene, that God will not permit this global genocide to succeed.

There will be nine more of our world conferences, God willing, before the curtain falls on this millennium. If you agree with the pope, I hope to see you at as many of them as God gives you the means to attend—and gives me the years to arrange. God bless you for helping to make Santa Clara an explosion of grace!

(As usual, HLI will make available the tapes of these excellent talks.)

Fr. Marx prays in his office while exercise-biking. "Most people spend their lives wasting them," he says.

Little ones such as this Singaporean child must be protected from womb to tomb.

Fr. Marx meets a happy young man with a handicap in Dresden, Germany.

At our national prolife conference in Manila in the '70s, Jaime Cardinal Sin concelebrates Mass.

Paul VI, the Pope of *Humanae Vitae,* to Fr. Marx, "You are a courageous fighter—never give up!" (Rome, 26 January 1973).

Praying for friends and enemies in HLI's chapel are concelebrants Fr. Barnabas Laubach, OSB, Fr. Matthew Habiger, OSB, Fr. Paul Marx, OSB, and pastor/chaplain Fr. Ray Mulhern.

Typical propaganda of the anti-life International Federation of Planned Parenthood (IPPF) in Nigeria.

Children are the only future a nation has (Lusaka, Zambia).

Teaching the multitudes on national TV in Zambia.

HLI was founded for families! California's Corcoran clan invades HLI.

Dr. Malachi Martin, banquet speaker at HLI's Tenth World Conference, with Dr. and Mrs. Bernard Nathanson.

Archbishop Roman Villalobos Arrieta of San José, Costa Rica with HLI youth educator Barbara McGuigan and Fr. Marx.

H.L.I. Goes to Eastern Europe

No. 82   July 1991

O n April 23, Father Matthew Habiger and I
journeyed to Rome to consult with various Church
officials and offer the Holy Sacrifice of the Mass
with Pope John Paul II in his private chapel. This
unforgettable Mass took place at 7 a.m. on the twenty-
sixth. I was given the place of honor, standing at the right
of the pontiff and reading the Gospel; Father Habiger
stood at his left.

His Holiness seemed extremely tired and haggard—
actually exhausted. But he met with each of us for a few
words after the Mass, as is his custom. "You are the
apostle of life," he told me. When I asked him to bless all
my benefactors, he said, "I pray for and bless all your
collaborators, all prolife groups everywhere." I presented
the Pope with my last three books, six prolife videos, and a
gift of $1,000. These gifts brought me a gracious thank-you
letter containing a second apostolic blessing.

H.L.I. GIVES "SILENT SCREAM" TO POPE

One of the videos I gave the pope was "The Silent
Scream." Imagine my surprise when I read that he told his
fellow Poles a few weeks later that he'd seen that film! It
"recorded a desperate defense by an unborn child in the
womb of his mother," he related. "It is hard to visualize a
more appalling drama."

Our little group, which included Marijo Zivkovic, our
coordinator in Eastern Europe, and Dr. Peggy Norris of
England, held a two-hour consultation with the staff of the
Pontifical Council for the Family. Then we took off by
rented van for Bratislava, the capital of Slovakia.

There, a year ago, Germany's Dr. Siegfried Ernst and I
sat with twenty medical persons to plan the future prolife
work for Czechoslovakia. We suggested a national seminar of leaders, and I offered to pay for most of it. Fortu-
nately, the ministry of health of the Slovak Republic
agreed to be the chief organizer and sponsor of what

turned out to be an international prolife congress. Several international groups joined, including the bishops' conferences of the Czech and Slovak Federal Republics.

The Bratislava meeting was a fantastic success: 1,800 people attended, and 200 had to be turned away. Cardinal Jozef Tomko, a Slovak who heads the Congregation for the Propagation of the Faith in Rome, opened and closed the congress with a High Mass attended by thousands and broadcast over national TV!

I told him that never before in twenty-eight years had I seen so many doctors, nurses, priests, seminarians, nuns, and bishops at a prolife conference. He pointed out that, sadly, the people of Central and Eastern Europe now want the consumerism of the West, with all the evils that affluence engenders.

Of Czechoslovakia's three provinces—Bohemia, Moravia, and Slovakia—the last is by far the most religious and most Catholic. But pornography, prostitution, divorce, "living together," and a host of other evils have arrived in Czechoslovakia and are taking root—not to mention Freemasonry and godless humanism.

People's first reaction to the lifting of political and socioeconomic repression is excess. Democracy often means

> ***People's first reaction to the lifting of political and socioeconomic repression is excess.***

freedom to see, hear, and do *anything*. When people have been enslaved for more than forty years, it's hard for them to acquire an understanding of liberty within the context of law and our fallen human nature.

POPE WARNS AGAINST WESTERN ILLS

For good reasons, the pope keeps pleading for "a new and necessary evangelization" in Europe; he warns of the very real danger that Marxism may now be replaced by "another form of atheism" that's no less a threat to Christianity. Worshiping liberty, Central and Eastern Europe seem "tempted by a vast, theoretical and practical, atheistic movement that appears to seek a new materialistic civilization."

Abortion is truly a plague. Slovakia's five million people induce 80 abortions for every 116 births; 3 percent of these are performed on unmarried mothers. Most abortions are done after two babies have been born. Bohemia's birthrate is 'way below the replacement level, but the Slovaks have two to three children per couple. Under the Communists, gynecologists had to perform abortions. That's changed; now they have to perform them only if the mother's life is alleged to be in serious danger.

The Church is battling mightily. Czechoslovakia has four seminaries, two of which are in Slovakia, where they're planning two more. Right now there are 400 major seminarians in Slovakia alone, sometimes living five to a room. All things considered, the Church stands a much better chance to recover in Eastern and Central Europe than in Western Europe. I'd say this observation is especially true of Czechoslovakia and Poland.

Hungary will have a harder time of it—despite the recent posthumous return from exile of her heroic Cardinal Jozsef Mindszenty, whose body was found to be incorrupt. Secularization is vast and deep in Hungary. The Christian Democrat Party commands only 6 percent of the vote and is a poor match against the Liberty Party and the Socialist (Communist) Party.

There are 90,000 abortions and only 105,000 births each year in this nation of ten million souls. Prostitution and pornography have sprung up everywhere. Sixty-five percent of the people are Catholic, and there are 200,000-300,000 Jews. The rest are Protestants of several denominations.

Thanks to low birthrates in the past, the percentage of old people and pensioners is exploding. The World Bank has insisted that retirement start at sixty-five rather than sixty, as a precondition for Hungary's getting loans. The helpless government knows that every year Hungary loses 40,000 citizens.

We're supplying zealous prolife doctors and budding prolife groups with much literature. The deputy head of the health ministry told me Hungary wasn't ready for a national prolife meeting but that HLI should cultivate grassroots activity. I'll have more for you on Hungary in a later *Report.*

Participants in the Bratislava conference came from eleven nations. It would be impossible to summarize the many talks. The great Italian prolifer, Dr. Silvio Ghielmi, gave me proof that the part of Italy where contraception is the most widespread has earned the highest abortion rate.

A French participant told me that in Paris one of every two marriages ends in divorce, *versus* one of three in the rest of France. Shacking up is common. The affluent French generate lots of sex but not enough babies to replace themselves. Meanwhile, they worry about the proliferating Moslems and mosques. The RU-486 abortion pill accounts for 55 percent of the reported child-killings; 80 percent of the legal abortions are paid for by the state, which refuses to pay for dental work or hearing aids.

PROLIFERS & CHURCH MAKING A COMEBACK

There seems to be a budding religious revival, though, especially among young people. The new bishop of Namur, totally prolife and energetic, leads the way. Other bishops seem to be waking up. Young people are reacting favorably to natural family planning (NFP) and are more curious than ever to learn the faith that's not taught in "Catholic" schools. I'll have a complete report on France for you in the future.

Marijo Zivkovic gave a great talk on Croatia, now free of her Red rulers. HLI's press in Croatia is now printing prolife and catechetical materials in ten Eastern languages, including our first Russian-language piece. Despite many abortions, Marijo revealed, the Croatian birthrate has reached replacement level; one priest's apostolate is to collect money from people in foreign countries to help Croatians have third children.

There are less suicide and divorce and more children in Croatia, proportionally, than in Switzerland, Germany, or Italy. The Communists were able to destroy the economy, the schools, and social and political life, but not the family or the soul. The Reds were too cowardly to have more than one child, but Catholics often had two (and many abortions, too, however).

I've met more genuine prolife medical personnel behind the crumbled curtain than in the whole Western world. By the way, a group in Czechoslovakia are publishing our *Love and Let Live* mini-brochure in their own language, as well as my *Eight Reasons Why You Should Consider Having One More Child.*

The tireless young Dr. Antun Lisec is all over Eastern Europe, giving talks and showing our films virtually every day to audiences of every description. In one area of Yugoslavia, he's been giving out pamphlets costing one-half cent apiece (which our friends' generosity pays for); the number of girls getting abortions has dropped 50 percent! Antun asked me to tell you that for every half-cent you contribute, you may save a baby in Catholic Croatia!

One great danger for Catholics behind the crumbled curtain is the false idea that contraception is the remedy for their massive abortion problem. I warned them again and again, giving evidence that contraception doesn't prevent abortions; in fact, the more contraception, the more abortions.

During the conference, various lecturers spoke to students in nearby medical schools. Dr. Siegfried Ernst performed superbly in two hours with these students. They were surprised to learn the difference between the atheist-materialist concept of man, where the human being is considered merely a biological, manipulable animal, and the Christian teaching that every man or woman is the priceless, valued image of God—or "God's property," as Cardinal Joseph Ratzinger observed recently.

We shipped much prolife literature and audiovisual aids to Bratislava in advance; on top of that, we brought ten boxes with us. I wish you could see how these truth-starved people snatch up our materials, having seen nothing like them. They're fascinated by our plastic models of twelve-week preborn babies, which will be seen by thousands.

Poor, good people! Victimized by forty-five years of Red tyranny, something we can't even imagine in the West— the incredible suffering, the cruel persecution, the inhuman tortures, the secret police everywhere, the snuffing out of religion and anything Catholic, wherever possible and by any means! You get a glimpse of it all when you speak to these people, who still believe, even

---

They know things about life that we've forgotten, things learned in the school of martyrdom.

---

though the West doesn't. They know things about life that we've forgotten, things learned in the school of martyrdom.

In Czechoslovakia, nuns are emerging from the underground and donning their traditional habits. Vocations are plentiful. Far more than 50 percent of the people go to Church every Sunday in this country, which is second in Europe to the USSR in abortions, proportionally. Czechoslovakia, a nation of almost sixteen million, has killed more than three million babies since the law was first weakened in 1950. The little ones lost all legal protection in 1986; abortions increased 28 percent over the next year. Last year 180,000 abortions and 210,000 births were reported. More Czechs died than were born.

H.L.I. CONFERENCE AIDS BATTLING POLES

Dr. Karl Gunning of Holland, who defeated the first Dutch abortion bill in the seventies and brought down the government over a vicious euthanasia bill last year, and Drs. Siegfried Ernst, Jr. and Sr., joined us at Bratislava. Now, with both a van and a car, our prolife team headed for Katowice, Poland, for another three-day seminar, loaded down with prolife materials. We couldn't have come at a more opportune time: the nation was in the throes of a passionate national debate over abortion.

In 1956, the Communists imposed virtual abortion-on-demand on Catholic Poland. Today, the Poles kill from

300,000 to 500,000 preborn babies yearly. Some 600,000 babies are born. Of course, the anti-Catholic, pro-abortion *New York Times* and the *National "Catholic" Distorter* brazenly assert that Poland records one million abortions annually. Whatever the true number, it's frighteningly high. It proves once more that when a nation casts aside "the common sense of history," whereby abortion was condemned in law, medicine, and religion, baby-killing becomes uncontrollable.

Questionable polls say that up to 60 percent of all Poles don't want to change the law. Because the doctors' income is very low, they kill babies privately to make extra money. And now taking hold is the false idea that contraception is the great remedy.

Earlier this year, Pope John Paul II endorsed the government's bill to restore legal protection to preborn babies. The Polish pope sees *Polonia Sacra* as a base from which to influence other nations behind the crumbled curtain. That is why he told Polish pilgrims to the Vatican, "We are convinced that this is not only a question regarding our nation, but of moving consciences in other nations" (*Washington Times*, 16 May 1991).

The pope gave three talks near the Polish-Soviet border so that he could make further inroads among the ten to twenty million suffering Catholics in the USSR, particularly the five million Greek Catholic Ukrainians, thousands of whom were allowed to flock across the border to see the Vicar of Christ.

In a powerful sermon at Koszalin, the pope asked his compatriots to set a moral example for the rest of Europe, which he said had "passed the stage of looking for God." To Poles of short memory, he thundered, "Never forget the God Who led you out of Egypt and the houses of slavery"— a reference to the Church's crucial role in ending four decades of Communist rule.

In Radom, he condemned abortion: "Land of my brothers and sisters! How can we continue to destroy the Polish family? We cannot speak here of liberty. This is the kind of liberty which makes man a slave!" "Bluntly, urgently and angrily," and with "both fists flailing" (*New York Times*), the pontiff compared abortion to the Nazi mass murders: "The cemetery of the victims of human cruelty in our century is extended to include yet another vast cemetery, that of the unborn, of the defenseless.... What parliament has the right to say: 'You are free to kill...'?" (What if spineless bishops everywhere began preaching like that?)

WILL BABIES REGAIN PROTECTION?

The Polish hierarchy has repeatedly condemned baby-killing, calling the Communist abortion law "an ally of evil." The Solidarity movement and President Lech Walesa also backed the Church-approved, no-exceptions, baby-protecting bill passed by the senate. It would impose jail terms on doctors who killed preborn babies illegally. But polls show there's a creeping anticlericalism; allegedly, the Church is no longer the nation's most trusted institution, having been superseded by the army.

The hierarchy has demanded that the separation of Church and State be dropped from the Communist constitution of 3 May 1990. Incidentally, the Polish constitution of 3 May 1791 was the first adopted in Europe and the second in history (after the USA's). Reds and other anticlericals accuse the bishops of wanting to make Catholicism the official state religion.

More than 90 percent of Polish citizens say they're believing Catholics. Last year, voluntary religious education officially returned to the government schools, thanks to the resented *fiat* of a government-Church committee. On 8 May 1990, the government stopped subsidizing the production of birth-control pills; the abortifacient IUD is the most common means of birth prevention. The ministry of health also decreed that abortions may now be performed only in hospitals, with the "permission" of four doctors. And doctors may now refuse to kill.

The *Washington Post* (14 June 91) reports that abortions have decreased sharply in Poland over the past year, mainly because of the Church's aggressive campaign against babykilling. Our benefactors deserve some of the credit: HLI has been supplying the Polish Church and prolifers with materials and advice for six years through our three branch offices there.

In mid-May of this year, leftish veterans of Solidarity and former Communists in the Sejm (the lower house) voted 208 to 145, with 14 abstentions, to delay action on the senate's abortion bill until after the October national elections. Bishops and prolifers had hoped to present the pope with the gift of the most protective abortion law in Europe during his nine-day visit in June.

The leader of the Sejm, Mikolaj Kozakiewicz, is none other than the president of Poland's infamous Planned Parenthood! (The shameful collaboration of PP with the Red fascists in many countries should be widely exposed.) Under the "round-table accord" that brought an end to Communist Party rule in 1989, 65 percent of the Sejm is made up of the hated Reds, who may be swept from office in the October elections. Thanks to the pope's appeals, abortion could still be outlawed after the new parliament is elected. But there'll be a long, tough fight; victory is by no means certain.

NEEDED: CHASTITY & N.F.P.

As always, the hardest task will be to change sexual habits, built largely upon abortion-on-demand since 1956. Like many North Americans, many Poles naively think the crucial task is to change the law. That would help, but it

---

Like many North Americans, many Poles naively think the crucial task is to change the law.

---

wouldn't cage the unleashed sexual appetite, which is supremely hard to tame.

That is why the teaching and promotion of the most neglected virtue, chastity—(along with NFP and a holistic marriage-preparation course)—is so vital in Poland, as everywhere. Besides, most abortions in the future will be microscopic, that is, induced early in pregnancy through drugs, at home. Thank God, England's Birmingham Maternity Hospital NFP Center (one of the best in the world) has trained more than 200 Polish teachers, with training programs under Sr./Dr. Elizabeth in Warsaw.

Over and over, we in the West hear and read that abortion is rampant in Eastern Europe because of a lack of contraceptives. A Czech physician at our conference vehemently denied this assertion, presenting facts. When I asked him about the quality of Czech birth-control pills, he retorted, "Good enough to export." Pills, he insisted, were plentiful because the government manufactured, promoted, and sold them. The whole question needs further investigation. I think it's a PP ploy.

We're trying to fill the many requests we received for pictures of aborted babies, posters, films, and video-cassettes. In some parts of Poland, our people have shown "The Silent Scream" on TV, plus four other prolife videos. Other TV stations will do the same, with your help. We're shipping the Poles more films and videos for broadcast.

We plotted and planned with editors, writers, and publicists. Our team laid plans for a shrewd, educational anti-abortion tabloid, 100,000 of which have now been published for key media people, writers, and teachers. We met many marvelous Catholic Poles, eager to do all they can to rid the country of the abortion scourge, which they see as a social disaster.

Besides "Planned Barrenhood," many foreign-funded feminist groups are fighting to keep the Reds' abortion law. These elements assert that banning abortion would create "a new kind of gynecological underground." They viciously attack the Church and the pope, saying, "...one totalitarian regime has replaced another and the Church is playing a leading role."

The pro-choice-to-kill gang tried to get parliament to hold a national referendum. There would have been five questions deciding whether abortion should be illegal in all cases or only in some. The bishops killed this clever, diabolical ploy.

"THANK YOU FOR TOOLS OF RESISTANCE"

Our three-day videotaped seminar in Katowice drew some 400 leaders from all over the country. It was a huge success. It focused directly on what Poles must do *now* in order to rescue their future from the tragedy of continued baby-slaughter.

Despite their poverty, Polish prolifers have started producing their own prolife literature, much of it imitating and adapting what we've sent them over the years. In long hours of discussion, we helped prepare them for the battles ahead.

Two bishops thanked me profoundly for HLI's contribution. Through its three branches in Poland, they said HLI had brought them the first "tools of resistance." I hope I can return for a week soon to fulfill many invitations to speak before the October elections and the vote on abortion. There's never enough time!

As you travel through the Polish countryside, you see huge, beautiful new churches going up, an eloquent witness to the Church's resurgence. The birthrate is barely at replacement level, though. And the number of priestly and religious vocations is down slightly in this, the only Western country producing missionaries, although the pope blessed a new major seminary in Koszalin.

The worst vices of the "democratic" West are moving in: prostitution and pornography from Germany, Denmark, and Austria; 100 sex shops; secular humanism, feminism, and so on. Poles told me that late-night TV now broadcasts raw pornography. So far, there's still no private TV or radio.

WILL POLAND'S ECONOMY RECOVER?

Economically, the thirty-eight million Poles have their backs to the wall, but, along with the Czechs, they still have the best chance of achieving a certain degree of recovery. The Poles have a deep Christian faith and a well-educated and orderly work force, and they learn fast. Again and again I was told how the brutal Soviets had raped them economically. That is why Poland lacks all kinds of farm and other machinery, and modern equipment in factories and mines.

Shelves in the stores are filled. But the goods are so expensive that most Poles can't afford them. The diet is dull. Horses and oxcarts sometimes crowd the roads. Once we saw three men pulling a cultivator steered by a woman. Meanwhile, Poland is earning high marks from the European and international business and banking communities for implementing private-property and private-housing laws, and for a pioneer program to dismantle the centrally managed socialist economy.

The government is concerned about falling exports and a slump in domestic production. Poland has devalued the *zloty* again (to 1,150 per dollar) to make her products more competitive abroad. Poland doesn't have the money to subsidize the return of 52,000 Soviet soldiers to the USSR, whereas wealthy Germany paid for new housing in the USSR, and other costs, just to be rid of the Red Army.

The Polish economy needs nothing more than foreign investments and credit; these seem slow in coming. The market economy is on course, especially now that Western nations, led by the USA, have forgiven Poland one-half of her huge foreign debt. But for the time being there isn't much for the ordinary people to be happy about: 22 percent —more than two million—are unemployed. Inflation has plummeted from last year's colossal 245 percent, but is still expected to reach 52 percent by the end of 1991.

The average monthly salary for workers is $150; pensioners get $85. One bishop told me that one big task now is to keep the people encouraged while they wait patiently for better days. Alcoholism is an enormous problem.

An interesting aside: the UN's World Health Organization (WHO) conducted an experiment using the latest means of chemical birth control on healthy women in an isolated part of southeastern Poland known for its health. Called the "Suwalki Eksperyment," it was stopped two years ago when Solidarity took over. The Polish doctor in charge of the experiment was handsomely rewarded with a trip to the USA, where he performs abortions to make more money.

Last time I promised you an account of our seminar and experiences in Lithuania and the USSR. Alas, I've run out of room. I'll finish the tale in the next *Special Report*. Meanwhile, please pray for Central and Eastern Europe!

Behind the Crumbled Curtain
No. 83   August 1991

We **had heard** how difficult it can be to cross the border from Poland into the Evil Empire; glasnost and perestroika haven't reached the frontier yet. But we had Dr. Helena Gulanowska with us, thank God, and so it took "only" two hours.

Helena was born in Vilnius, Lithuania. Her brother was shot by the Communists at age eighteen; her family eventually migrated to Poland. Because she had already crossed the border nineteen times to lecture on "Christian culture," she knew which guards were reasonable. Once over the border, we saw two miles of cars waiting to cross into Poland from the USSR; the red tape and harassing/delaying tactics are so bad that sometimes people are held up for twenty-four hours!

I thought we'd never reach Vilnius, Lithuania's capital. As we drove through the night into another time zone (the immense USSR has thirteen of them), we observed virtually no traffic. Hitting the potholes in the road kept us awake. We'd been warned that the water wasn't fit to drink. The bottled mineral water tasted strange. Food was scarce and unappetizing.

We finally arrived at our destination in the predawn darkness and found lodging in a poorly lit hotel formerly used by Red officials, where services taken for granted in the West simply don't exist. (After hours of frustrating walking and waiting in Krakow, we'd received visas for the USSR only at the last moment. Later, we found out they were good only for Lithuania, although we drove through Byelorussia.)

Together with a very helpful Lithuanian health department, HLI co-sponsored a two-day prolife seminar attended by 500 people, including many doctors. Nuns in habit were on hand, as were priests. Everyone was warm, friendly, and most cooperative.

Lithuania has a population of almost four million; before the Soviet takeover, virtually everyone was Catholic. Vilnius has 600,000 inhabitants. The per capita

income is 6,380 rubles ($2,000-3,000, depending on the
ruble's fluctuating value); 40 percent of the people are
involved in industry and construction, 21 percent in
agriculture and forestry. The national product is 4.7
percent industrial and 22.6 percent agricultural, much of
the rest being service-related.

The friendly Lithuanians date themselves back to the
first century. Lithuania, however, was founded only in
1236. Christianity was established in 1387. During World
War II, the country was occupied in turn by the Germans
and the Soviets. The Reds never went home, thanks to the
Nazi-Soviet pact that divided Eastern Europe into spheres
of influence. By the mid-1950s, the Communists had
deported 800,000 Lithuanians to Siberia, including clergy,
religious, and Catholic leaders.

LITHUANIA REBORN—BARELY

The Lithuanians like to tell you that the independent
republic of Lithuania was re-established on 11 March 1990
by the Popular Front. In 1988, thanks to the gradual
easing of oppression under Gorbachev, the Catholic
Church regained its central position in the life of the
people. Today the Church prints a biweekly national
newspaper and other publications.

Reluctantly, the Reds returned beautiful Vilnius
Cathedral, which they'd confiscated and turned into an art
gallery. Cardinal Vincentas Sladkevicius of Kaunas
emerged from twenty-one years of house arrest to offer the
first Mass for 20,000 people. In 1989 Pope John Paul II
quickly appointed bishops to fill vacant dioceses. Defiant
priests and nuns invaded the schools to teach the faith. On
3 November 1989 a new Lithuanian constitution replaced
the old Soviet version.

But then, on the night of 13 January 1991, the Red

---

*The tenacious Lithuanians are
absolutely certain they'll be a free
people in the future.*

Army took over the radio/TV and press buildings. In
surrounding parliament, which was defended by "people

power," they killed at least 14 people and wounded 678 (the Western media never reported the latter figure). Every Lithuanian was prepared to die on that horrible night. But the tenacious Lithuanians are absolutely certain they'll be a free people in the future.

The population is 79.6 percent Lithuanian, 9.4 percent Russian, 7 percent Polish, and 4 percent other nationalities. The birthrate is barely at replacement level. The official number of babies aborted is 50,000 per year, but doctors think the true figure is 100,000—at least 130 every day. Married people obtain most of the abortions. The chief means of birth control, besides surgical abortion, are the Pill and the IUD.

Within Lithuania's 26,173 square miles are six dioceses with 670 priests and more than 1,000 nuns. Priests, bishops, nuns, and lay leaders suffered horribly for their faith. I offered Mass at the oldest church in Vilnius, St. Nicholas, which had been built by a German businessman in the fourteenth century. I preached in German, with the pastor translating.

During the persecution, the Communists authorized only twenty-three seminarians, all of whom had been interviewed and approved by the KGB. The KGB often invited these candidates for the priesthood, during their seminary training, to collaborate. Boys weren't allowed to serve Mass; the godless Reds knew this activity might spark a desire to become a priest. (Defiant U.S. bishops and pastors who allow "altar girls" don't seem to understand that.) Today 225 seminarians are studying in two seminaries. Father Habiger, Dr. Gulanowska, and I had a great time addressing these young men one afternoon.

Today 80 percent of the people are Catholic. There are some Russian Orthodox; the Lutherans have seven small churches and the Baptists four. The Seventh-Day Adventists and the Pentecostals have one church each. The Moslems have two mosques and the Jews two synagogues, but no rabbi. From Sweden and the USA has come a well-funded Pentecostal sect that is very aggressive and quite successful in working with the youth.

As for the other Baltic countries, Estonia is mostly

Russian Orthodox, having only 10,000 Catholics. In neighboring Latvia, where a low birthrate and large-scale Russian immigration have reduced the proportion of Latvians to barely 50 percent of the population, about 30 percent of the latter are Catholic. There's one Catholic seminary. Unlike the Lithuanians, the Latvians must depend on ethnic minorities to shed the Communist yoke.

A CHURCH ON THE CROSS

In these three martyr countries, every third priest was imprisoned; many were tortured, and some were killed. "How great is the need for Lithuanian priests," the pope moaned in Poland, for this "Baltic bastion of the Church."

Viewing Lithuania's beautiful, majestic, but dilapidated buildings and her many churches turning gray from disrepair, one can only imagine her former grandeur. After forty years of neglect, many churches are in perilous condition, because the Soviets had prevented all but the most basic repairs.

But far worse is the damage done to people's faith. One bishop lamented, "The fact is, many people have practically no idea of the Christian faith. They make the sign of the cross when they go into a church but know no prayers or hymns. Nor do they know even the simplest things about their religion."

Local TV was on hand to videotape interviews with all of us. One of Lithuania's chief gynecologists had attended our symposium in Bratislava, Czechoslovakia; he came home to declare that Lithuania's young gynecologists will never again learn how to perform abortions. The effects of these seminars are incalculable! Three Catholic doctors from Latvia are already plotting a seminar with us for this fall.

From Vilnius, we went to Lithuania's second-largest city, Kaunas, a center of magnificent Catholic history and culture. After chatting with gentle Cardinal Sladkevicius, we held a long session with major seminarians. We'd already been sending them prolife materials, which they use well. We met with various Church groups and arranged to ship them things they need after enduring so many years of painful deprivation. It was hard to leave the warm and long-suffering Lithuanians who, like the Poles, have Catholicism in their bones (their churches were overflowing on Sunday). By the way, young Lithuanians now learn English instead of Russian.

PRIEST GIVES "MARX"-IST LECTURE

It was another long journey from Kaunas to Grodno, a city of 200,000 and the capital of Byelorussia, a republic of ten million. Some of Byelorussia once belonged to Poland. Here the Polish/Russian Catholics and Yugoslavia's great Marijo Zivkovic had organized an evening seminar at a medical research center of 300 students and doctors.

This seminar turned out to be a unique experience: what does an American Catholic priest whose name is Marx, in a black suit and Roman collar, tell a group of Russian medical students and faculty, with a huge statue of Lenin staring him in the face? I prayed. I prayed again. Then, in my talk, I took the tense audience around the world, describing the medical situation concerning contraception, sterilization, abortion, and euthanasia. They seemed absolutely fascinated.

The research center provided two translators. One was excellent; the other called me "Father." At the end, the audience asked so many questions that we had to cut it short. They wanted to know about contraception, sterilization repair, AIDS, abortion in the West, the age at which people marry in the USA, euthanasia (which several participants thought OK, as long as it was requested), and "overpopulation."

I had some fun with the last: after giving the facts about our empty earth and its enormous untapped resources, I told them, to their seeming delight, "Karl Marx, my namesake, although really no relation, maintained that the 'overpopulation' problem was a function of capitalistic, economic, and social injustice. And he was right." Dr. Gulanowska and Marijo Zivkovic also addressed the group, receiving good responses.

I learned that every Soviet medical student must learn "scientific English" (400 hours over ten months) "because 60 percent of the world's good medical literature is in

English." Soviet doctors, 75 percent of whom are women, make less money than construction workers.

After the seminar, our hosts gave us a party featuring finger sandwiches, red horseradish, tea, candy, coffee, vodka, and cognac. Marijo is a genius at proposing toasts and relieving tension with jokes. Sufficiently liquored, the two stiff Communist commissars on the staff finally imitated him in proposing toasts. I secretly poured most of my drinks into two empty coffee cups.

Once more, I saw the wisdom of the old saying "In vino, veritas" (although there's some truth in beer, too, they say). Thus, one commissar, learning that my birthday was near, grabbed the beautiful silver samovar and told me, "We Russians don't have much, but what we have, we give away." Today this handsome gift stands in our HLI library for all to admire.

It took forty minutes for us to check into a neighboring hotel that night, only to find out that because our visas were valid only for Lithuania, we couldn't stay there. Bureaucracy: delay—wait—suffer—*caramba!* Finally, some enterprising Pole sneaked us into a room. Neither Father Habiger nor I slept well. He was ill-disposed (Brezhnev's revenge) and thirsty. We couldn't drink the tap water, and we couldn't buy the awful-tasting mineral water because every shop was closed. We were rescued by a generous Polish woman who sneaked us two cups of tea from her home.

RUSSIA'S FUTURE PRIESTS

Strangely, last fall the Reds returned to the Church of Grodno more than 100 parishes, plus an old, run-down, but large seminary. They also gave back the cathedral, which the medical school vacated for this purpose. The pope quickly appointed the young, highly educated Tadeusz Kondrusiewicz as bishop; he lost no time in starting a seminary. Now, forty-three major seminarians from all over the USSR attend.

Father Habiger and I had the priceless privilege of addressing them for three hours. All were neatly dressed in black cassocks. But their shoes were in sad condition. The building was run down beyond your imagination. The seminarians are fixing it up as much as they can, and they prepare their own meals. The desperate Communists forbid any volunteers; the rector must use union labor. He must also pay in foreign money, preferably dollars, for which he gets a poor exchange of rubles.

Bishop Kondrusiewicz has since been appointed archbishop of Moscow. Before the pope agrees to visit the USSR, he's appointing bishops as fast as he can in order to reconstruct an embryonic national hierarchy. What a hero's welcome he'll get from the estimated 12-30 million Catholics, and from others, too! The clever Gorby will try to milk the occasion for all he can.

Russian Orthodox Church officials won't be pleased. Stalin gave them all of the Catholic Church's property after they capitulated to him—something no Christian in the USSR has forgotten. Today, the Orthodox find it pain-

---

The Orthodox find it painful to give churches back to the Eastern-rite Ukrainian Catholic Church.

---

ful to give churches back to the Eastern-rite Ukrainian Catholic Church. The tensions are many and acute.

Grodno has about fifty elderly Byelorussian priests, plus a contingent of Polish priests trained in Poland for this eventuality, for a total of about 110. The rector of the seminary was an old, infirm Georgian; it was obvious he'd suffered much for Christ. He told us this was the last seminary between Europe and the Pacific Ocean, and that he needed at least $300,000 to repair it.

These great Grodno priests now function freely in many parishes even outside the diocese, starting catechism classes, caring for the sick, fencing with the Reds, and so on. Their stories left an indelible impression on all of us. I gave the rector my last $100 bill. Thinking of my bene-factors' great generosity, I promised him more and assured him that HLI will adopt his seminary. His seminarians need so much. There are now four Catholic major seminaries in the USSR, with 300 students. How many students are there in *your* local seminary? Huge Boston can claim only thirty-five!

Since 1985, Russian Orthodoxy, the USSR's largest religion, has seen the number of its parishes grow by 63 percent; Catholic parishes have grown by 30 percent. There are 11,118 Orthodox parishes and 1,385 Catholic. Moslems, Jews, Baptists and Seventh-Day Adventists show similar growth. There are an estimated ten million abortions in the USSR every year, but the many children of the fifty million Moslems hold up the Soviet birthrate of 2.3 per family.

Secret decrees that clamp down on believers and restrict public worship simply aren't obeyed in the chaotic Soviet Union today. Church schools are allowed, and religion can be taught in public schools as an optional subject. Atheistic propaganda has ceased. The regime now accepts the idea of religious conscientious objection to military service and is working on a law allowing alternative service. Last May 22-24, a Catholic-Marxist dialogue in Moscow, co-sponsored by Vatican and Soviet organizations, revealed that there are 52.4 million Orthodox Christians and at least 12 million Catholics. (The papal nuncio, Archbishop Francesco Colasuonno, estimates there are thirty million Catholics, not including seven million Ukrainian Catholics.)

THE FUTURE: EXPLOSION OR REVOLUTION?

In this enormously resource-rich land, where there's surplus food here and there, the transportation system is so primitive that the food rots. The USSR is loaded with oil and gas, but her pumping machinery is decades behind the times. The great Father Werenfried van Stratten once told me it'll take 100 years to straighten out Russian society and the economy. When I mentioned this prediction to a trusted Russian, he shot back, "No, not even then."

I asked my Russian friend whether he trusted Gorbachev. "No way. He's a Leninist bureaucrat—that means *apparatchik* to you." Said another, Gorbachev is a "dyed-in-the-wool Communist, a Socialist; he is a good foreign diplomat but is beholden to the generals and the KGB."

In Western Europe, the great fear is that if Gorbachev fails and is deposed, political wars will shatter this mammoth empire, leaving 30,000 atomic weapons up for grabs—or triggering military intervention by Moscow to re-establish "order" at home and in nearby lands. A gigantic, uncontrolled emigration would flood Western Europe. Many thinking Europeans fear this development; their affluent, soft, babyless life would come to an end.

And that's not all. Thinking Western Europeans believe their young people wouldn't resist a Soviet invasion. Pacifism is strong. Many young people have no will to fight, being selfish, materialistic, and godless.

There are many things I cannot tell you for fear of endangering confidants in the USSR. We must always distinguish between the forty million Communist Party members (or former members) and the enslaved people, who are very earthy, poor, and somewhat damaged psychologically after eighty years of inhuman treatment, with no experience of freedom. No wonder the USSR has sixty million alcoholics, a broken-down medical system, bribery, much thievery, no experienced managers, no tradition of private property, no established markets—and history's greatest bankruptcy. Meanwhile the pornography and other crud of the godless West slithers in.

I keep thinking, "Let's make the 11,000 Marxist professors who infest our American colleges and universities, and the Red sympathizers in Congress, Hollywood, and our news media, spend six months in the USSR so they can feel for themselves what it's like to live in the 'people's paradise.' Maybe they'd like to help excavate some of the USSR's 100,000 mass graves."

Our four outstanding HLI seminars in Bratislava, Katowice, Vilnius and Grodno have shown us how to conduct these conferences in many cities behind the crumbled curtain. We can hold them even in the USSR. We must do so in other countries, such as Hungary, Romania, and Bulgaria. How those people need your help!

WILL LOUISIANA'S LOOPHOLE BILL WORK?

Last year the legislature of very Catholic Louisiana passed a law banning all abortions. Maverick Governor Buddy Roemer vetoed it, and the lawmakers almost overrode his veto.

This year the bishops of Louisiana (supported by the National Right to Life Committee, or NRLC) entered the battle full-force with HB112-SB3, a bill that came to be called the "Bishops' Bill." They asked every Catholic legislator for exceptions in cases of rape, incest, and life of the mother.

Apparently they thought the governor would veto a no-exceptions bill and that the lawmakers wouldn't override a veto. Also they may have thought the U.S. Supreme Court would uphold only an exceptions law. But it's an enormity for Catholic bishops to assert that the law may allow some innocent citizens to be killed. A *Washington Post* editorial and four secular columnists saw the illogic of making exceptions—if some babies can legally be killed, why not others, they asked?

Keep in mind that Louisiana's civil and criminal codes protect unborn children as persons from the very beginning; the Bishops' Bill repeals that legal personhood!

Notre Dame's Professor Charles Rice, ex-abortion provider Carol Everett, yours truly, and others testified against the bishops' abortion-restriction bill. Everett, who had run two lucrative abortion mills in Texas, explained eloquently that abortion had nothing to do with rape, incest, or life of the mother, and *everything* to do with the greed of the abortionists. Dr. Rice presented the legal fine points. Julie Makimaa, who was conceived in rape, dramatically reminded the legislators that if the bill could be retroactive, they were considering a vote to have her killed.

The bishops' loophole bill says one thing but does another. It pretends to prohibit abortion, yet it specifically provides for the killing of unborn children in certain cases. It says it's the policy of the State of Louisiana to protect human life from the moment of conception but then qualifies that statement by saying "to the greatest extent possible." Then it fails to provide that protection, by specifying certain classes of human lives that may be killed.

How did the bishops and the NRLC decide "which categories of unborn babies were eligible for this

---

> **Maryland's Frederick Post:** *How did the bishops and the NRLC decide "which categories of unborn babies were eligible for this sacrifice?"*

---

sacrifice...?" cooed a writer in Maryland's *Frederick Post* (27 June 1991), who accused them of "moral inconsistency" and "political expediency." To the embarrassment of the bishops, Governor Roemer immediately wanted to include "defective" babies and others.

HOLES IN THE DAM

I pointed out that nowhere in the world has an exceptions law worked. Such laws have always led to abortion-on-demand. A few holes in the dam will sooner or later wash out the whole structure.

Abortionists everywhere have an ingenious capacity to exploit exceptions. Jane Hodgson, the notorious Minnesota abortionist, has testified under oath, "A medically necessary abortion is any abortion a woman asks for." There's no practical way to police the abortionists.

Only Right to Life of New Orleans supported the Bishops' Bill. Every other prolife group in Louisiana opposed it, as did other organizations. Prominent in resisting the loophole bill were the prolife Baptists and their great, Thomas More-like leader in the legislature, Woody Jenkins.

While Jenkins's no-exceptions bill was bottled up in committee, Governor Roemer vetoed the Bishops' Bill. The lawmakers then made Louisiana history by overriding a governor for the first time in this century.

Next, Jenkins called for a concurrent resolution to knock out the rape and incest exceptions. For this, only a simple majority vote was necessary, and the governor couldn't veto it. The bishops had said from the very beginning that they'd support both bills, thus making it easier for the legislators to choose the loophole bill. But their support of both bills now seems, in fact, not genuine. They refused to support Jenkins's resolution. No doubt, they thought they did the right thing. Perhaps the future will prove them right. But I doubt it.

With astonishing naiveté the bishops argued that out of 15,000 legal abortions in Louisiana last year only four were performed for rape and incest—so the exceptions law would save all the other babies! They also said that every year they'd support efforts to tighten the law by removing the exceptions. But Jenkins's resolution gave them the chance to do so this year. They refused.

Obviously, abortion is such a hot potato that no legislator will want to re-fight this war year after year, session after session—as was proven by the anger that greeted Jenkins's attempt to remove the rape and incest exceptions. For two days he tried to contact New Orleans' Archbishop Francis Schulte to solicit the bishops' support, but to no avail. They could have had what they said they wanted in the beginning: no exceptions.

Behind all this questionable maneuvering was the inconsistent NRLC. They've now left their trail of tragic failure in eight states, while Connecticut and Maryland have written abortion-on-demand into *statute law*. In the process, NRLC has emasculated the prolife legislators, who should never start with exceptions, even if that will be the best, perhaps, that one can vote for in the end.

VICTORY IN COLOMBIA!

In *Report No. 76,* I described how the international abortion forces were trying to put abortion into Colombia's new constitution. We gave permission to a prolife youth group, VIVE, to reprint our most successful prolife pamphlet, *Love and Let Live,* in Spanish, as well as our shocking "Freedom of Choice" poster and postcard showing the severed head of an aborted baby. They produced 30,000 of the pamphlets and 50,000 of the pictures and plastered them all over Bogotá, the capital. Prolife members of parliament showed them to undecided colleagues. The result: abortion was voted down! Colombia became the eleventh country where HLI and our friends have helped to lick the deathmongers. Thank God and thank you!

Watching the Swiss

No. 84   October 1991

I **went to a dying Europe** March 4-13 to speak on life issues at the new branch office of the Pontifical Council for the Family at Rolduc, Holland, and at St. Peter's Seminary in Wigratzbad, Germany. I also went to inspect a building kindly offered to us for a new HLI branch in the small village of Cernay, France. City authorities are eager to give this abandoned church-and-office complex to HLI to keep it out of the hands of the Moslems, who want to turn it into a mosque. Yet another purpose of this mission journey was to organize a new HLI branch in Stans, Switzerland—our thirty-eighth.

SEMINARIANS' POSITIVE RESPONSE

My talk at Rolduc was postponed till some future date. At St. Peter's Seminary in the diocese of Augsburg, I spoke three times to the seventy-three seminarians, showing them two abortion films. The seminary was founded to bring back followers of the late Archbishop Marcel Lefebvre after he went into schism.

Of the seminarians, fifty-two are French, ten are American, and the rest hail from Switzerland, Germany, and Holland. Although students are housed three to a room, the authorities have had to turn down a number of candidates, having already received thirty-five applications from the USA alone for next year.

The Society of St. Peter wants to establish a seminary in the USA, but many U.S. bishops have rebuffed it. Why? Apparently, because of fear of Latin, of a return of pre-

---

The Society of St. Peter wants to establish a seminary in the USA, but many U.S. bishops have rebuffed it.

Vatican II teachings, of reinstating the old Mass, and of too many young Americans' joining a seminary guaranteed to be orthodox.

I found the seminarians a happy, healthy lot. They responded heartily to the prolife/profamily message. I tried to paint them a picture of the world in which they'll have to carry on their priesthood, a world fallen back into a new, hedonistic paganism. I left them films, videocassettes, and literature, with more to follow—all provided by the generosity of our friends.

THE FOLLY OF LOOPHOLES: A CASE HISTORY

The beautiful, mountainous, landlocked country of Switzerland has attained the highest standard of living in Europe, but also the most HIV/AIDS cases, proportionately. The disease is spread the same ways as elsewhere in the West, except that historically the Swiss have had a high number of homosexuals. The Swiss are afflicted with drugs, loose sexual morals, and hordes of tourists who like to sample the local flesh—plus that of many taxpaying, legal prostitutes imported from Asia. With 6.6 million people and more than a million "guest workers" (mostly men), every sixth inhabitant is a foreigner.

On 21 December 1937, the Swiss passed a law allowing abortion for a "serious" danger to the mother's life or a "great" danger to her health. Of course, these loopholes expanded to virtual abortion-on-demand. Switzerland soon became the abortion haven of Europe, if not the Western world. I recall Swiss gynecologists' telling me in the early seventies that pregnant French women would get off the train and head to the nearest gynecologist to have their babies killed.

In 1971, the Society for Free Abortion (*Verein für straflosen Schwangerschaftsabbruch*)3 promoted abortion-on-demand for the first three months of pregnancy. The people rejected this policy in a referendum in 1977. In 1985, the powerful Yes to Life (*Ja zum Leben*) organization sponsored a solidly prolife referendum. This, too, lost, the media being brutally pro-baby-killing. I was involved in both battles.

Today, more than 90 percent of Swiss abortions are

performed for psychiatric reasons: an unintended
pregnancy, failed contraception, change of mind after

**Today, more than 90 percent of Swiss
abortions are performed for psychiatric
reasons.**

---

intentional pregnancy, pregnancy from spousal or date
rape, the slightest suspicion of a "defective" child,
pregnancy from fornication or adultery—these and many
more reasons have become "psychiatric grounds" for
abortion.

In short, to kill a preborn baby legally, a Swiss doctor
must find "an indication"—in this case, an allegedly
serious threat to health or life, verified by two other
doctors, neither of whom may perform the abortion. Of
course, there are no genuine medical reasons to kill unborn
children, and so doctors freely induce abortions for "health"
reasons, mainly mental. Because psychiatric excuses for
abortions are rare in other countries, I conclude that the
Swiss psychiatric profession is rather primitive!

The supposedly "tight" laws to control abortion in
Switzerland and New Zealand are proof positive that the
National Right to Life Committee's and the U.S. bishops'
"exceptions" bills won't work. Such laws have stemmed the
tide nowhere, and they won't stem it in the USA, where
they've already failed in several states, leaving abortion-
on-demand written into statutory law in Connecticut and
Maryland.

It's ridiculous to think that by allowing some
abortions—say, for rape, incest, and life of the mother—we
can curtail the unique problem of abortion. It's even more
naive to assume that we can tighten up the law every
year—the "incremental approach." Besides, the moral
forces in today's society are too weak to support a loophole
law.

The abortionists can always exploit or invent some
loophole. Then the burden falls on the state to prove the
abortion wasn't legal—something other countries have
refused to do because of court costs, failure of police to

report, lack of witnesses, and so on. And once some preborn babies have been classified as expendable, we've sacrificed the fundamental right to life of all babies, no matter what eloquent words or phrases are used to explain the classification.

Ireland, where all abortions are forbidden, supplies proof that medicine doesn't need abortion to protect women's health. In fact, Irish women, who still give birth at all possible stages of life, are the healthiest women in Europe! A few Irish mothers do die in childbirth, but these deaths cannot be predicted, and, in any case, legalizing abortion wouldn't prevent them.

No one knows how many baby-killings take place in wealthy Switzerland; the number often given, 20,000-30,000, is far too small. There must be vastly more abortions than that, considering how low the birthrate is. For secrecy, some women still go to England, Austria, or Holland to secure their uterine murders. Thanks to watchful prolife doctors, three of Switzerland's twenty-six cantons forbid abortions in hospitals. But unscrupulous and greedy "doctors" perform them in their offices by "D and C," suction, or "menstrual regulation"—the last being early abortion by mini-suction. (In Holland, they call this procedure "overtime treatment"; it's never reported as an abortion, but the state pays for it all the same. Meanwhile, the Dutch pretend they have achieved the lowest abortion rate in Europe.)

The Swiss have two powerful, well-organized, and well-financed prolife groups, *Ja zum Leben*, which is mostly Catholic, and *Helfen statt Töten* (Helping Rather than Killing), in which Protestants predominate.

BISHOPS *VS.* VICAR OF CHRIST

All knowledgeable Catholics agree that the Church in Switzerland is, for all practical purposes, in moral schism, perhaps in worse shape than Germany's Church. (Some of Germany's wildest theologians are Swiss, e.g., Hans Küng and the notorious Father Johannes Böckle, who left plenty of their kind behind in Switzerland.) During Pope John Paul II's visit to Switzerland, the Swiss hierarchy embarrassed him by having lay people distribute most of the Communions while scores of priests sat idle near the altar.

Three years ago, rebel priests and religious tried to cancel the pope's choice to head the important diocese of Chur, which also includes Switzerland's largest city, Zurich. When 42-year-old Bishop Wolfgang Haas was to be consecrated in the cathedral, scores of protestors physically blocked its entrance. What the disloyal "Catholics," priests, religious, and even some fellow bishops have done to oppose, frustrate, or oust Bishop Haas is unbelievable; I'll tell you more in the future.

Bishop Haas's crimes are loyalty to the pope and the magisterium, insistence on private confession, adherence to *Humanae Vitae,* letting no women live in the seminary, and just about everything else that Modernist theologians have discarded or twisted "in the spirit of Vatican II."

While I was in Switzerland, the Swiss bishops were preparing to go to Rome to see what they could do about "the Haas affair." (Only one Swiss prelate, the bishop of Rorshack, is pro-Haas.) Modernist theologians speak contemptuously of the "Haas Case." Incidentally, about a year ago, the Swiss hierarchy *did* issue an orthodox statement on sexual morality. But they didn't require priests to promote it; the theologians played with it "in the spirit of Vatican II." Please pray for Switzerland's bishops, priests, religious and Church—especially Bishop Haas.

SWISS FOUND H.L.I. BRANCH AND MORE

On a happier note, thirty enthusiastic prolife leaders, many of them doctors, attended a five-hour meeting at Stans to found HLI's thirty-eighth international branch. It will function under the able and courageous leadership of a magnificent prolife gynecologist, Rudolf Ehmann (his masterpiece, an exposé of the abortifacient character of Pill and IUD, can be ordered from HLI for $4 postpaid).

It was a blessing to see some of the pioneers such as Mr. and Mrs. Lagrange of Bern, with whom I'd worked to build a resistance to abortion in the seventies. We all agreed that we'd failed, but we're consoled that God won't ask us whether we succeeded, only whether we really tried.

The Swiss have established an excellent, organized natural family planning (NFP) program, thanks to Swiss doctors and our friend Dr. Josef Rötzer of Austria. One

---

The Swiss have established an excellent organized natural family planning (NFP) program.

---

doctor alone, Margaret Reck-Wallis, has trained eighty "multiplicators." They supply excellent literature and periodicals and, for the size of the country, a good number of trained teachers. A group of Swiss doctors recently organized a worldwide interfaith network, the International Association of Physicians for Natural Family Planning (IAPNFP), with which HLI hopes to collaborate.

IAPNFP doctors prefer to speak of "natural fertility regulation" (NFR) rather than natural family planning, which they think smacks of the amoral, antilife Planned Parenthood (PP). According to the doctors' guiding principles:

> IAPNFP considers NFR methods an essential element of a philosophy of life whose hallmark is fully integrated, unconditional conjugal love. NFR forms an ideal basis both for dialogue between loving spouses and for responsible parenthood. The transmission of the understanding of NFR fulfills an important role in the field of education in human love and sexuality, beginning with young people and extending to the married couple and the family, the primary unit of every society.

These good doctors are persuaded, as I am, that contraception leads to abortion and that it destroys youth, family, Church, and state. They wonder, as I do, why more bishops, priests, and religious don't see the obvious. Meanwhile, prolife Swiss doctors insist that NFR is nature's way and therefore God's way: in any one menstrual cycle there's time for God (fertility) and time for man (infertility). Man should not usurp God's time, especially because man's time is so much longer.

The Swiss birthrate is so low that if the million-plus foreign workers walked out some afternoon the economy would collapse (neighboring countries are in a similar fix). The Pill, IUD, and sterilization are present everywhere. Doctors told me that the Pill and IUD are harmful to women's health but that these effects are minimized, overlooked, hidden away, and never mentioned by the medical profession. The same is true of post-abortion syndrome (PAS), which is very real; HLI has introduced our abundant PAS counseling literature to Switzerland. As in other countries, sex "education" and the condom represent the overoptimistic, foolish hopes for curbing AIDS. Switzerland is beautiful on the outside but rotting on the inside.

THINGS THEY DON'T TELL YOU ABOUT NORPLANT

For months, you've heard and read, on TV and radio, in editorials in the *New York Times* and in national news-paper columns, about the great "contraceptive" subdermal implant, Norplant. The developer and promoter of this abortifacient is the abortion-pushing, Rockefeller-funded, New York-based Population Council, working through its International Committee for Contraceptive Research. To prevent lawsuits, Norplant is manufactured in Finland.

What you *haven't* been told is that *Issues in Reproductive and Genetic Engineering* (III, 11-28 February 1990) has published a devastating critique exposing the lies and deception surrounding the testing of this potion.

Norplant consists of six matchstick-like storage rods, which supposedly feed into the user's hormonal system a steady flow of chemicals for five years, for virtually perfect birth control. The Norplant promoters assert, without evidence, that after surgical removal of the rods the user's system regains its normal reproductive capacity. The less you believe of what you've read about Norplant, the more truth you'll know. Here's a synopsis of the journal's exposé:

Trials of new contraceptive drugs and
devices continue to be undertaken by
family-planning research organizations on
poor women in developing countries. They
are being carried out as if the drugs being
tested were part of the regular family-
planning program. Consequently, the
subjects of research do not get adequate
information about the real status of the
drug and believe they are accepting
approved contraceptives. In so doing, the
ethics of biomedical research are violated.
Not only do the women serve unknowingly
as guinea pigs in a medical trial, they are
subjected to an unsafe contraceptive as a
means of population control.... Investigation into the Norplant trial in
Bangladesh highlights gross violations of
ethics, an inadequate research practice, and
a lack of care for the health of the women to
whom Norplant was administered.

That's putting it mildly. None of these poor, illiterate
women were told that this was an experimental drug; none
were told that no one knew the consequences of using it;
none were told that they were, in fact, human guinea pigs.

Duly rewarded "motivators" were paid to persuade
women to subject themselves to the foreign contraceptive/
abortifacient imperialists. Many women weren't even
examined before the six silastic rods were implanted in
their arms; they weren't told that it's more difficult and
expensive to dig them out than to implant them.

LET 'EM BLEED

Advertisements touted Norplant as "a wonderful
innovation of modern science." Claims of effectiveness were
incorrect, and, of course, the women were never told they
were inducing microscopic, early abortions. Even
hemorrhaging women had to beg for a long time to have
the rods removed.

According to medical ethics and the Helsinki Accords

of 1975, a volunteer testing a new drug should know that it's on trial and that he will be compensated for any damage it causes. But unscrupulous birth-control researchers have set themselves above medical ethics or international declarations.

In all the hoopla about "this great implant," none of the volunteers were told that as many as 39 out of every 100 Bangladeshi women demanded removal of these abortifacient, drug-oozing rods. Nor were they ever told that only young, healthy, and nonsmoking women were used as guinea pigs. The results were compared mainly with the data from women who used the Pill, instead of with data from healthy women who used *no* hormonal contraceptives. This pseudoscience went on and on.

When the Norplant experiment started in 1981, such an outcry was raised against the false advertising and the blatant disregard of women's health that the international contraceptive-drug merchants halted the experiment, only to return with less controversial methods in 1986.

Who was involved in Norplant? Besides the Population Council, most likely the U.S. Agency for International Development (USAID), the UN Fund for Population Activities (UNFPA) and super-abortionist Malcolm Potts's tax-fed Family Health International of Raleigh, North Carolina.

The abortifacient imperialists had a similar experience in Brazil, where the parliament recently passed a resolution demanding an investigation of foreign depopulation groups. They've sterilized 40-50 percent of all women of childbearing age in that Catholic country! This policy has caused a dangerous fall in the birthrate. Particularly guilty are PP, known locally as BemFam (Benefit the Family), and USAID. (Why aren't you reading this in the Catholic press?)

Dear friend, this is what your tax dollars are doing in the poor countries of the Third World, where both Church and mankind will find their future. Newspaper editors, reporters, columnists, and the electronic media lie to you. What I've said here is only the tip of the iceberg. For more information, read our new bimonthly *Population Research Institute Review* (send $20 for your subscription).

SIX REASONS FOR NO VOCATIONS

The number of vocations to the priestly and religious life is a measure of the Church's health in any nation. Since Vatican II, vocations have dropped 91 percent in the USA!

> *Worldwide, 100,000 priests have abandoned their commitment, including more than 12,000 priests in the USA.*

Worldwide, 100,000 priests have abandoned their commitment, including more than 12,000 priests in the USA. Likewise, 25,000 nuns have walked out. The median age for the remaining sisters is sixty-five, with one-third of the total being retired.

Almost 200 U.S. seminaries have closed. Since 1980, the number of U.S. seminarians has declined by 43 percent, from 13,000 to fewer than 7,000. Meanwhile, the Catholic population has increased markedly, although some fifteen million baptized Catholics don't attend Mass regularly or have joined other religions.

One reason for these disasters is that today we rarely, if ever, pray for vocations as we used to do in the old days, despite the former abundance of priests and religious.

Another reason is that among the estimated thirty million babies killed by surgical abortion since the late sixties, there were at least 5,000 future priests, 10,000-12,000 future nuns, and hundreds of future brothers. Remember, the Church depends on its babies.

Meanwhile, sterilization has become the most common means of birth control among Americans, including Catholics. Among U.S. couples married ten years or more, or having two children, at least 30 percent have used this veterinarian's approach to birth control. Surely, unless they reform, such parents aren't capable of cultivating vocations. The typical U.S. couple engages in plenty of sterile, contraceptive sexual activity, but has barely two children. Its philosophy of "A boy for you, a girl for me, and heaven help us if we have three" is no seedbed for vocations. And will these selfish parents be willing to surrender their son or daughter to a seminary or a novitiate? Don't bet on it!

In 1946 seven million Catholics attended Catholic schools; today, fewer than three million attend "Catholic" schools, most of which are no longer truly Catholic, judging by their graduates' religious illiteracy. Have you noticed how many pro-abortion public officials and others leaders are graduates of "Catholic," often Jesuit-run, colleges and universities?

Once, Catholics tended to marry Catholics; today, 17 percent of Catholics are married to non-Catholics, a rate twice that of their parents. Studies show that mixed marriages rarely produce vocations, that priests and religious come mostly from larger, middle-class, often somewhat struggling families headed by deeply believing parents.

"Shacking up" used to be rare. Today, more than two million U.S. couples live in that "alternative lifestyle." Does anyone expect vocations to come from such fornicating, contracepting shackmates? Nor is the staggering amount of early "sexual activity," often triggered by "sex ed" courses or "family-life education," conducive to fostering vocations.

Then there's the scandal of some 200 priests and even some bishops who are guilty of homosexual acts and pedophilia—for which the Church and her insurance carriers have had to shell out an alleged $300-500 million in damages. This scandal is no advertisement for the priestly life!

And what about the condition of the seminaries in this country and throughout the Western world? Many parents ask me where there's a safe seminary to train their son; others say they wouldn't send their boy to *any*. As Cardinal José Falcoa of Brasilia has remarked, "Seminaries have lost the sense of the sacred, and have become mere hostels—havens for questionable, dissenting theologians." Please pray!

A PRIESTLESS BOSTON?

Everywhere in the USA we see the decline of the Church. In Los Angeles, thirty-five priests left the priesthood this year, about three times the number of men ordained.

Recently I preached at all the Masses and gave an evening talk in a suburban Boston parish. The median age of priests in the 400-parish archdiocese of Boston is sixty-two; only 120 are under forty. At one time the seminary had 622 seminarians; today there are only about 75. The archdiocese once ordained 89 priests in a single year; this year they ordained 13. Next year there'll be 8.

Every "Catholic" congressman and senator from Massachusetts votes for abortion. Former Knight of Columbus Ted Kennedy is surely one of the worst. Massachusetts is about 50 percent Catholic; why do they vote for these killers? Why haven't bishops and priests taught their people that just as not one hair falls from our heads without God's knowing it, so every single vote for a killer politician must be accounted for at the Last Judgment?

Recently the bishops of Massachusetts issued a pastoral, "Family, the Key to Healthy Society." I showed it to our staff to get their reactions. All were astonished that the bishops said nothing about contraception and sterilization, little about euthanasia, nothing about "sex ed" (although they suffered a big scandal over it recently), nothing about deadly homosexuality or pornography, and nothing about marriage preparation. I have only admiration for Boston's beleaguered Cardinal Bernard Law, whom the media and rebel "Catholics" attack mercilessly. But surely it's fair to ask what's happened to once-Catholic, Irish Boston, and why Massachusetts' Catholics are so blasé about baby-killing.

We Get Letters

From Angola

We are very grateful for your attention to us. God bless your intentions and your efforts.

Our country is very much influenced by Communist ideology. Abortion is very commonplace and frequent, contrary to the traditional morality of Angolans.

Your movement can help us prepare young priests to fight the antilife mentality, and so we accept your offer to send us materials.

> Seminario Bom, Pastor
> Benguela, Angola

From Austria

Thank you very much for all the information you sent. Sometimes it seems to me that it is impossible to do productive work for the unborn when so many obstacles keep turning up. Once I have overcome one, others appear to block the way. I think a snail must travel faster than I do with my work. I want nothing but to give my voice to unborn babies! Please, Father, keep on praying for me!

> Christine Derfler
> Steyr, Austria

From Brazil

To Magaly Llaguno: Just knowing about you makes me very happy. I have this friend in a distant land, with the same targets and feelings about people and the entire world.

Still, I also feel very lonely, since in the city where I live I'm practically alone in my prolife interest. I think that others don't consider this matter important enough to be reflected about. To people here it makes no difference whether someone is living or someone has been killed; it's absolutely the same thing to them. But to prolifers it *isn't* the same!

By the way, it's always good to know that when the baby gets through the tube to the womb it takes him up to three days to choose the exact place where he will stay. It is not just *any* place that will satisfy him!

Tarcisic de Barros
Joinville, Brazil

From Burma

I am a spiritual director of the St. Aloysius Seminary, Pyinoolwin, of the Archdiocese of Mandalay in Burma. I got your letter and pamphlets from St. Joseph Major Seminary here. I studied in Rome. I am thirty-one years old and have been in the priesthood for eight years.

I am interested in your apostolate and want to join you. Many priests from Burma have never been outside the country and have no knowledge of or interest in abortion, which is practically nonexistent here. I myself, however, know the danger of abortion and contraceptives and know they will soon come even to us. Already I have noticed some sales of contraceptives in our black market.

Our bishops seldom go abroad, and none of them have studied in other countries; so they do not know a lot about what is going on outside our land.

I have been organizing a group of fourteen young priests to cooperate in our apostolate, which includes the education, support, and adoption of poor children. I secured some financial help while abroad and am spending it on this venture. Our group meets every month to plan what we can do for the Church of God. I shall explain the danger of abortion and contraception; later we shall organize the seminarians.

Please pray for our success. The Catholic Church here forms just 1 percent of the total population of 40 million people. We are indeed a silent church with no contact, no help, no activities. All our schools were nationalized twenty-eight years ago, and missionaries were expelled.

Most books never reach us, especially in large shipments. So please send two or three each time, but no video tapes yet. I would also love to know a seminary professor, especially a professor of Scripture, who could guide and help me intellectually.

Rev. John Aye Kyaw
Pyinoolwin, Burma

From Czechoslovakia

Hello! How are you? I am a 19-year-old boy, a medical student in Kosice.

Why am I writing to you? I should like to be a pediatrician or a psychiatrist. I saw the picture "Freedom of Choice?" (a head of an unborn child) and obtained your address from this picture.

I have spoken to a large number of people who told me that the artificial interruption of pregnancy is a normal thing if the parents don't want the child. I know it *isn't* normal, because the fetus is a human being.

I'd like to lead a war against induced abortion. I can talk about these things to my friends and other people, but I haven't any printed material on the subject. Can you send me some pictures and other material? Have you any information about worldwide and U.S. statistics? It would be very good if you would send me cheap materials, because my parents aren't rich. I wish you good luck.

Daniel Farkas
Kosice, Czechoslovakia

✠ ✠ ✠ ✠ ✠

I am pleased to inform you that with the help of Human Life International and of you personally, Father, we have founded a family center in Brno. The main task of its medical department will be natural family planning.

Your visit with Marijo Zivkovic helped us to initiate this activity, and your financial gift enables us to cover our initial expenses and traveling expenses of cooperating physicians. Thank you for all your support.

Vojtech Cikrle
Bishop of Brno,
Czechoslovakia

From England

I am a Catholic priest of the Diocese of Leeds. At present I am associate research fellow at the Linacre Centre for Health Care Ethics in London. For some months I have been engaged in research on eugenics and its influence on modern social and medical policy and clinical practice.

It seems clear to me that the whole antilife movement has many of its roots in the ideology of eugenics and the eugenics movement. This is now such a commonly accepted popular everyman's philosophy that we may easily overlook the fact that it has gained prominence through the activity of powerful pressure groups and a process of social engineering. Its origins, growth, and effective triumph can be identified and described in terms of its leading thinkers and their academic, social, and political activities. Its influence on medical practice and health-care strategies is especially worth investigation. It seems that the Holy Father and his best advisors are keenly aware of the presence and the pervasive force of this ideology through such bodies as the International Planned Parenthood Federation, which has been listed annually for decades as a member of the British Eugenics Society.

I am convinced of the need, as you yourself have stressed, for the education and formation of prolife priests. I find that priests are sometimes the most resistant to the prolife apostolate, a fact that is deeply distressing and painful for certain other priests (and upsetting to laypeople involved in prolife work).

Fr./Dr. John C. Berry
London, England

From India

Thanks so much for the parcel of books, posters, and pictures that we received recently. We are using the material to full advantage in our programs for the young and the not-so-young.

On June 23 (1990) our National Association for Respect for Life conducted a program for principals and teachers of schools, teacher-training colleges, and junior colleges, attended by 250 participants from sixty institutions. In August we held an inter-collegiate cultural festival featuring competitions in creative writing, debate, extempore, role play, painting and sketching, poster-making, and music. The festival's theme was "The Girl, You Are Precious," and it was a real success.

In November we will be conducting similar competitions for school children of upper grades. We bring out very forcefully the preciousness of life.

Sister M. Annuntiata
Bangalore, India

✠ ✠ ✠ ✠   ✠

Thank you immensely for all the valuable material that I received just the other day. Be sure that I will remember you that the Lord bless your ministry and the humble work that we do here on your behalf.

The rate of abortions here is something colossal. Considering the population that we have, having an abortion is of no more consequence than having a tooth pulled. To make it even easier, clinics are close to most of the brothels; it makes the work so much simpler.

Human life here is so cheap. The people do not know what to do with this child or that child. They even go to the extent of putting their children into accident-provoking areas to have them intentionally injured, sometimes fatally, in order to get some money for their families.

Abortion in the United States is so refined in comparison with that in India. You have to see it to believe it. We are trying your methods of sensitizing our youngsters to this great sin. Pray for us, Father Paul, and if your organization can help us with material from time to time we shall be grateful.

Rev. Ian Doulton
Bombay, India

✠ ✠ ✠ ✠ ✠

Thank you for your continual generosity and munificence to ALERT (Abundant Life Education Research Trust). You have sent us books, pictures, videos, etc. All these have helped us to educate our people and have certainly saved the lives of many babies. I hope you will continue blessing us, as we do need help.

This year one of our auxiliary bishops, Rt. Rev. Bosco Penha, who visited us a short while ago, has encouraged the parish priest at St. Michael's to allow us again to expose thousands of people, both Christians and non-Christians, to the true facts about abortion. A weekly novena to Our Lady of Perpetual Succor is held every Wednesday. We will be putting up posters and distributing leaflets to the seventy or more thousand people who will be attending the novena. Please do remember us in your prayers.

Kevin L. Fernandes
Bombay, India

From Indonesia

I am very grateful for your kindness. I have received the books and pamphlets you sent me. They are very useful because I am working now in the field of pastoral care of the family in our Archdiocese of Semarang, Indonesia.

Artificial methods of birth control are used in the family-planning program in Indonesia, except for abortion. That does not mean, however, that in our country there are no induced abortions. In Indonesia induced abortion is both illegal and culturally prescribed! No apparent efforts are made to invoke moral and legal sanctions against those known to have procured abortions. Many hospitals in Indonesia routinely offer (abortifacient) menstrual-regulation procedures.

To emphasize the family-planning program, the Indonesian government has already set plans in motion, both as to motivation (by targets, incentives, and education) and as to the participation of society. By supporting me in my work you could save many babies in Indonesia. Your participation is needed. May God bless you and your efforts.

John Hardiwiratno, MSF
Semarang, Indonesia

From Japan

I'm totally against abortion under any circumstances or for any reason. Because of pervasive educational and political beliefs, most Japanese have been led to believe that abortion is sometimes necessary to protect the life of the mother and therefore should be acceptable. But I have learned from reading some Catholic publications from Ireland (through which I learned about you) that their belief is not at all true, considering the innocence of the child and the actual safety of the mother.

In this anti-Christian country where obscene books and suggestive TV programs are abundant and prostitution is practically legal, there seems to be almost no way of protecting the lives of unborn babies. The worst of it is that no Japanese Christian churches have strong convictions against abortion or do anything to fight against it. Most Japanese consider abortion just the means of solving the failure of contraception.

I have never joined any kind of group either in Japan or in foreign countries. But at this time I've been so greatly astonished and distressed by the cruelty and immorality of this world that I would like to join an organization that is fighting against abortion. As my first step I wish to learn how prolife Catholics are conducting this fight, possibly in the USA or Europe, where many Christians have become perverted in their ideas about life. Please give me your suggestions about what I should do. I pray for your good fight.

Takehide Abe
Tokyo, Japan

From Kenya

It is unbelievable!

At Kiambu Hospital, every two or three months, they ask the doctors from the Lions Club to perform sterilizations on a group of women (twenty to thirty) to whom they have given appointments. The service is free, the patient paying only ten shillings for the hospital bed. I do not know how much counseling or information they give the women before the operations.

Two weeks ago a Kenyan doctor told me that he himself does an average of fifty tubal ligations per week!

Sister Josephine Albertini
Nairobi, Kenya

✠ ✠ ✠ ✠   ✠

Our Family Life Counselling Association of Kenya is at rock bottom as regards finances! We are hoping our many projects will go through this year despite the fact that it is a very, very slow process. Since USAID stopped funding us we have been struggling with innumerable difficulties; still we are surviving and feel God is with us and that our work will bear much fruit.

I would be very grateful if you could send us more materials. Our shelves are depleted after we distributed and reprinted a lot of your handouts at our stands in five provincial agricultural shows in 1990. Please also send any books you think would help us.

Sister Stanislaus
Nairobi, Kenya

From Mexico

I write these lines to thank you for the newsletters in Spanish which you have been so kind as to send me. The information and testimonies presented are very valuable, and they are of great help to those who read this material.

Please send me any pertinent information about the results in countries where abortion has been decriminalized, as well as news about the United States. If you have information such as this available about other countries in Latin America, I should appreciate your sending it to me.

May the Lord continue to bless you and your apostolate.

> Monsignor Adolfo A. Suarez Rivera
> Archbishop of Monterrey
> Mexico

From Myanmar (Burma)

Thank you very much for your letter and also the *HLI Reports* and *Special Reports*. I have been working as a volunteer lay missionary for twenty-two years. I do not get a salary, but the good Lord sees to it that my family and I live. I have six children, the oldest being thirteen years old.

I agree with your efforts to save unborn children. Even in Burma, now called Myanmar, people think that abortion is something like smoking a cigarette, They have lost the sense of sin, especially with regard to sexual sins.

This is the first time I have heard about a man who works so hard to protect human life in the womb. I want to know more about your work. But I am a poor jungle missionary and will not be able to pay money for your publications. I shall try my best to spread word of your mission, teach the people, and write about prolife ideas. I really hate abortion. I shall fight with all my might this bad enemy that destroys the character of our young people.

> Patrick Kham Vai Lian
> Kalemyo, Myanmar (Burma)

From New Zealand

The picture of St. Joseph that you sent out is, we all think, the most successful representation of St. Joseph that we have ever seen. It has a touch of genius about it. To show Our Lady resting and the strong young St. Joseph holding the Christ Child is a unique concept.

H. P. Dunn, MD
Auckland, New Zealand

✠   ✠   ✠   ✠   ✠

Enclosed is a contribution from the Society for the Protection of the Unborn Child (SPUC) for the Yugoslav doctor you mentioned in a recent report. You say that Dr. Antun Lisec wants to give up his medical practice and work full time for the babies of Yugoslavia. We trust this gift will give him some financial, as well as moral, support toward his inspiring work.

Our own John O'Neill send his regards. He is working tirelessly for the prolife cause here in New Zealand and thinks that very soon he will be in a position to prove beyond doubt that every abortion performed here is illegal.

If you and the members of HLI and your subscribers could include his work in your prayers it would be wonderful.

Mark Devereux
Dunedin, New Zealand

From Nigeria

Last night I wrote you asking for posters for the prolife Sunday we are planning in this parish. Today a box of cassettes, tracts, and small posters arrived! I am very grateful. The photograph entitled "6-7 Week Baby" is fantastic. Thank you for your helpfulness.

Rev. Thomas K. McDermott, OP
Yaba, Lagos, Nigeria

✠ ✠ ✠ ✠ ✠

I gratefully acknowledge the receipt of the very helpful materials you are constantly sending us for our work in the diocese and other parts of the country. I thank God for the great gift you have not only of making easy contacts with people and places but also of writing and producing volumes of rich material to make your apostolate very effective and tremendously fruitful.

I am greatly indebted to you for your many kindnesses to us in many ways, and I pray that God may continue to bless and reward you in your great endeavor. Be assured of our prayers for greater success in your special apostolate to protect the sanctity and dignity of human life.

Dominic Cardinal Ekandem
Catholic Diocese of Abuja
Garki, Abuja, Nigeria

I am writing to acknowledge receipt of the VHS tape "The Silent Scream." It's wonderful of you. Dr. Nathanson's investigation is quite a revelation. It caused a stir in our studios the day I had the materials dubbed onto the u-matic tapes we use in the studios. Arrangements are being made to air the program to over three million viewers.

Matthew Otalike
Nigerian Television Authority, Nigeria

✠ ✠ ✠ ✠ ✠

Yesterday we had our first prolife Sunday in this parish, and it was very successful. On every wooden post (there are seventy) in the church building we stapled the color posters you had sent us. The bulletin had a prominent prolife theme. Every sermon was on abortion (six sermons by six different priests, some Nigerian and some American). After Mass, the altar boys handed out the little pamphlets you had sent. Mr. Lawrence Adekoya showed the film "Abortion: A Woman's Decision" after every Mass to packed crowds.

Definitely we made an impact yesterday. I thank you for the supportive role you played. To my knowledge no other parish in this archdiocese has ever had a prolife Sunday. Perhaps we will inspire others to do the same. We have sent a packet of information to the archbishop.

Incidentally, young people wanted the posters at the end of the day to bring back to their high schools and universities to show their friends. Many of them requested copies of our sermons. You are very lucky to have Mr. Adekoya; he is a gem.

Father Thomas K. McDermott, OP
Lagos State, Nigeria

I returned from my ten-day trip east of the Niger last Sunday and went on two shorter trips almost immediately. Since then I have made another three-day trip to Asaba. All were fruitful trips, with requests to come back.

Everywhere I go there is another invitation to reach out further, and this emphasizes for me the importance of training more people to handle this important prolife task. The limiting factor is not likely to be men but materials. I think it might be useful to spend money more on slide projectors and appropriate slides to save costs: you can't provide cine projectors for everyone.

One thing is certain. The battle to enlighten people is enormous, just as the incidence of abortion, quietly proceeding, is enormous. Everywhere I go, priests confirm this conviction. The bishop of Awka said to me, "You have done more apostolic work in four days with your film than we have been able to do in years of preaching from the pulpit. You must come back to the university campuses."

> Lawrence A. Adekoya, KCSS
> Human Life Protection
>   League*
> Ijebu Ode, Nigeria

*An HLI affiliate

✠ ✠ ✠ ✠ ✠

By the special grace of God, the professional personnel and students in this hospital have started to ask to have full professional courses in NFP leading to instructor certification in NFP. I had just run such a course, mostly for senior nursing and midwifery students, of which twenty completed the course last December. We plan to run the course three times each year.

Please send me actual learning texts and manuals for NFP—as many as you can send. Also, I should appreciate receiving specific prolife animation literature in large numbers; we will use some of these in our adolescent youth congress which comes up in May each year.

M.C. Asuzu, MD
Ibadan, Nigeria

✠ ✠ ✠ ✠ ✠

I wish to express my profound gratitude to you for the work you are doing for God. Your visit to Nigeria last year, which was given wide publicity in the news media, made a great impact on so many people. It really helped to clear some doubts and expose the obnoxious works of Planned Parenthood.

Please send us some books and pictures that will help people to learn the truths and operations of natural birth control. They will be displayed in our library for the general public. We believe that this gesture will help people to come to grips with the realities of life.

Romanus Ajala
Imo State, Nigeria

I am a student of the National Missionary Seminary of St. Paul and have always supported the fight against abortion. I got some copies of "Love and Let Live" from a friend here. The people I showed it to felt shocked.

Please send me as many more copies as possible. I want to make others aware of what abortion is.

Ambrose C. Obioha
Nigeria

✠ ✠ ✠ ✠ ✠

The propaganda about population explosion and the need to drastically reduce it has reached us in Nigeria through the media and the government policy. All sorts of organizations promoting artificial birth control by condoms, pills, and IUD have been allowed tacitly to operate in the country. And government has come out with the policy that each woman is limited to four children—a policy that has generated controversy. Some have rejected this policy because it is against the law of God. Others rejected it not only because it is against the law of God but also because it is against our cultural norms (and we do know that our cultural norms derive from our limited knowledge of God). Others have rejected the policy because it contains a dangerous seed of political and religious implications.

Religiously, the policy of one woman to four children favors the Islamic religion. A Moslem man is allowed to marry up to four wives, which means he can beget sixteen children—four from each of the four wives. But a Christian cannot have more than one living wife, which means he cannot beget more than four children from this one wife. What happens after the fourth child is born is clear to everyone. The couple will have no choice but to resort to condoms, pills, IUD, and, indeed, sterilization.

What it means in the final analysis is that there will be more children for the Moslem families than for the Christian families. The policy is, indeed, the most dangerous and effective Jihad in Nigeria, because it seeks to wipe out the Christian religion and implant Moslem religion in Nigeria. Father Marx, we need men like you to open our eyes and give us some encouragement.

Julius Bishung
Lagos, Nigeria

From Papua New Guinea

I have to confess that I was shocked right down to my boots when I looked through the materials you sent and saw the photographs of aborted babies. I suppose we lead a fairly sheltered life here. Abortion has always been practiced in our traditional society, using "bush" medicines and treatments known to some of the women, but it has always been a deeply shameful thing, a hidden thing, a thing not spoken about. It is not legal in our country, thank God, but artificial birth control is. This is *not* traditional in society here and is very repugnant to many of our people. Nevertheless, artificial birth control is pushed strongly by our health department, as is sterilization.

In our diocese we have a husband-and-wife team (Gabriel and Catherine Sianot) who are employed full time conducting family-life enrichment courses. I am sharing your materials with them, and they are extremely grateful. They have a hard time getting hold of textbooks and teaching aids of any kind. They teach NFP to our people in the villages and have totally disproved any idea that it can be understood and used only by literate and well-educated people.

Their magnificent work is poorly supported by the diocese. Our resources are so limited and funds are simply not available. So if you have any other materials that they could use, please be assured that these things would be of inestimable value to them.

Father John M. Glynn
Tuias, Papua New Guinea

From the Philippines

Recently the Family Planning Organization of the Philippines received a grant from the Department of Health to further support its programs for "responsible parenthood." Again the devil is at work. Obviously, the government approves of such programs. However, we are not discouraged, nor will we tolerate it.

We have been encouraging many people to react by writing to different newspaper agencies and other forms of media against such policies being implemented by the government. I have to say that the "silent majority" needs to be heard; otherwise the fight against this outrage will continue endlessly.

Do you not agree, Father, that what makes a person believe in contraception is the lack of doctrinal formation? Ignorance is the greatest enemy we have in front of us. It is only through proper Christian education that one can realize the beauty of God's creation.

Ana Maria A. Capistrano
The Philippines

Warm greetings from Mindanao! I received the box of rosaries and the box of books. I cannot thank you enough for all these precious things. The materials on breastfeeding and natural family planning are very timely, as I am lining up my subtopics for my seminar lectures on family welfare. I am emphasizing the health hazards, not just the immorality, of contraceptive devices and sterilization.

I am working with four couples who bore children after they had been told they were sterile. Their only shortcoming was that they were unable to recognize their fertile periods before instruction. They are so grateful!

> Sister Marie Marthe Orencio
> Mindanao, Philippines

From Puerto Rico

For some time now, I have been interested in your "parish notes" and would appreciate receiving this vital service. If a Spanish edition is available, it would be a Godsend!

My work is all in rural areas. The people in Puerto Rico are badly infected with the contraceptive mentality so strongly laid down by the sterilization drive a few years ago. Many were astonished when I informed them that contraceptives are sinful and not permitted. I have tried to teach natural family planning, but it is difficult because of my limited Spanish fluency and even more limited material.

Puerto Rico offers excellent pre-marriage instructions, well formulated and presented by our family institutes, but after marriage there is little to nothing on a pastoral level available from these sources. Support for NFP is almost impossible without constant reinforcement at the parish and diocesan level. Many of our priests privately acknowledge that contraception is a sin, but they never preach it or mention it in their talks on sexuality or morality. Many priests even condone contraception or sterilization, ignoring the moral and heroic values of NFP!

Still, I remain hopeful as more and more videos and printed materials become available in Spanish from sources I know to be authentically Roman Catholic. May God bless you.

Father Daniel P. Ewald
Jayuya, Puerto Rico

From Slovakia

I received parcels of books and other materials from you. Thank you very much!

There is an unbelievable lack of information about the miracle of prenatal life, not only in the Slovak population but also among "experts." People are very grateful to receive this information. Many times it is really eye-opening for them.

The last part of your brochure on prenatal development is devoted to the horror of abortion. We can also stress the fact that it was the Communist regime that did not allow people to hear this information and forced them into obtaining abortions. It is educational to show the women the real facts about the tragedy of their "emancipation"—which has been, in truth, their slavery.

Joseph Glasa, MD
Bratislava, Slovakia

From Southern Africa

I am rector of St. Augustine Major Seminary here in Lesotho. I write briefly to thank you, Father, for your Godsent letter and informative materials about the existence of HLI in the USA. I am deeply impressed and send you my profound congratulations for having founded this work.

I received this material just as I was arriving from a Lesotho conference on the AIDS epidemic. I had just told the delegates the stand of the Catholic Church on the importance of chastity before marriage and the Church's rejection of the use of contraceptive devices.

I am a staunch supporter of prolife activities. It really consoles me to hear about your work; I feel a part of it. We want to belong to it. I am now showing my staff and students this beautiful document on prolife seminarians that you have sent us.

Rev. Dr. Pascalis Mokhethi
Lesotho, Southern Africa

From Sri Lanka

Thank you for your letters and for the two packages of literature I recently received.

Please consider my request for TV, VCR, and a photocopier when HLI finances permit. I realize the financial strain you are faced with, having to fill the requirements of so many countries around the globe.

The Family Planning Association of Sri Lanka has been functioning from the beginning of the 1950s. It has had the blessing of every government that has come into power since 1948. The World Bank first insisted that the government reduce the population in order to receive financial assistance in developing the country.

The family planners have their headquarters in Colombo and have opened offices in almost all of the provinces. Their propaganda slogans are carried on state envelopes, TV, and radio. The most popular slogan is "A small family is golden."

The FPA has trained all the medical officers and midwives attached to the health department; they in turn advise married women who come to the clinics to adopt contraception. Midwives visit the homes of families and advise everyone to control the family size. The Pill (under the name "Mithuri," meaning "female friend") has been put on the market. Condoms are readily available, and we could see even children inflating them like balloons. Abolut fifteen years ago vasectomy was introduced into all government hospitals; people of either sex were paid to have sterilizations done.

In predominantly Catholic areas the FPA used the Lions Clubs to get around the clergy. These clubs donated money for social services to the churches and got members of various church associations to go out visiting homes and speaking to people about "small golden families." They passed out handbills claiming sterilization to be 100 percent successful, the Pill 75 percent, condoms 50 percent, and NFP 25 percent. Not surprisingly, the people went in for sterilization. Whole Catholic villages got sterilized, and by the time the Church hierarchy awoke to the facts, the damage had been done.

It is the majority race, the Sinhalese, that has most gladly accepted contraception. The Muslims have kept away from it altogether, and their numbers are increasing rapidly. Now the FPA is maintaining its staff throughout the area to make sure that its achievements are not disturbed.

Bede N.A. Perera
Wennappuwa, Sri Lanka

☩   ☩   ☩   ☩   ☩

Compliments to Human Life International!

I have been reading your publications on human life. They are of immense help to me as the rector. Thanks ever so much.

Human Life International is rightly termed a prophet from God for the world today. Let its voice echo and re-echo in every nook and corner of the world, not only to be heard but to reach all hearts and be lived.

May the Lord bless you and your apostolate!

Father Rector
Haputale, Sri Lanka

From Tanzania

How I cherish reading the *HLI Reports* and *Special Reports!* I get to learn things I never knew. One is shocked to see that some shepherds of the Church are lining up with abortionists in one way or another!

Dear Father Marx, you are indeed the Apostle of Human Life Protection. God bless you in your great apostolate. I wish you abundant graces in your noble mission.

James D. Sangu
Bishop of Mbeya
Tanzania

The latest literature you sent me helped a lot in my NFP coordination work. I happened to contact somebody dealing with the population-policy committee and gave her some prolife pamphlets and past symposium handouts. She passed them along to members during their five-day meeting addressing the same issue. They were very grateful to receive the information, and the meeting ended in postponing the population-policy draft.

Please send more literature, as the battle is continuous.

Maria G. Kato
Tanzania

✠ ✠ ✠ ✠ ✠

Greetings from the St. Charles Lwanga Senior Seminary! Please accept our heartfelt sentiments of gratitude for your HLI newsletter and reports, which we now receive regularly. The information contained in your reports is most enlightening and helps us to assess our lecturers on these pressing moral issues of today. Our seminarians will soon start their own group of Seminarians for Life at Segerea.

Father Vedastus Rugaijamu
Dar es Salaam, Tanzania

From the USA

I'm one of your biggest fans! Your newsletter is so informative and convincing that God, through your efforts, has converted my husband and me to being not only prolife but anticontraception, mainly from reading your newsletters.

We were both cradle Catholics, but now we are *real* Catholics. The only problem is that after three children and a vasectomy in four years, we converted after the fact. I wonder whether you could print some encouragement and advice for those of us who have already made the *big* mistake.

We have been to confession, but how else do we deal with our wrong decision? What does the Church say? We are sad that we didn't receive better instruction before we were married. We pray for others, that they will be more fortunate.

God bless you—you are an inspiration!

No name if you print this, please.

(Name withheld)

✠   ✠   ✠   ✠   ✠

I'm twenty years old and torn up by the unbelievably widespread, seemingly unchecked mass-murder of the innocents. To me, all life is sacred. To think that abortion in most cases is legally and socially acceptable is very frightening.

Never have I been confronted with such a strong case against abortion than when I encountered a huge graphic poster showing an aborted baby's decapitated head being held by tweezers. This image brought home the ugly reality of abortion more strongly than any amount of lectures, speeches, or statistics could ever accomplish.

Johnny Bruit
Stockton, California

Concerned with the lack of teaching traditional Catholic doctrine in local parochial schools, last September a group of devoted Catholics opened a small school, Sacred Heart Academy, with ten students. We hope to double the enrollment this year, as parents learn the truth about the diabolical sex-education and AIDS-education classes mandated by the cardinal-elect Mahoney for their innocent children.

We provide an excellent academic education. In the Iowa Basic Tests, version 1974, that our students took last month, they scored an average of two grades higher than their school grade.

> Delores (Mrs. J.L.) Dautremont
> Simi Valley, California
> Phone: (805) 527-9161

✠ ✠ ✠ ✠ ✠

Your latest *Special Report* shook me up—as you can tell from the enclosed check. Please send me three copies of your AIDS booklet.

You are deeply admired!

> Monsignor Joseph D. Munier
> Santa Cruz, California

✠ ✠ ✠ ✠ ✠

I'm only thirteen but would never think of doing such a barbaric ritual as abortion. I think I would rather die myself than live the rest of my life full of guilt and shame.

There are many people who try very hard to have children and would go through a lot just to experience

the joy of raising them. Why do others, when they
have the chance of making two people very happy
and giving the baby to a loving home, take his life
away instead?

> Ramonda D. Hibdon
> Delhi, California

✠ ✠ ✠ ✠   ✠

Here's the prayer to St. Joseph the Worker that I told
you about—edited to bring it close to the original
version:

> St. Joseph, patron of all who are
> devoted to work, obtain for me the
> grace to work in the spirit of penance,
> in order to atone for my sins; to work
> faithfully, putting duty before my own
> desires; to work with gratitude and joy,
> considering it an honor to use and
> perfect the talents I have received from
> God; to work with order, moderation,
> peace, and patience, without shrinking
> from weariness or difficulties; to work
> with a pure intention and with
> detachment from self, having ever
> before my eyes the hour of death and
> the accounting I must give of time
> poorly spent, of talents left fallow, of
> good left undone, and of empty pride in
> success.

This seems to me one of the most nearly perfect
prayers I've ever encountered. In moments of near-
panic, I get great help from recalling the words "with

order, moderation, peace, and patience."

Patrick Riley
Washington, D.C.

✠ ✠ ✠ ✠ ✠

I am eighteen years old and am writing to you because I am very much opposed to abortion and would like to become involved and help somehow. Please send me any information your organization has, and I'll do my best to pass it along.

Anna Marie Naples
Sarasota, Florida

✠ ✠ ✠ ✠ ✠

After our son was born in July 1990, I decided to put your pictures of aborted babies up on the big wall at our place of business. Many people fill out forms at a counter by this wall and thus see the photos. I really can't tell you how much good they have done.

Today, for example, a policeman looked at the pictures. He told me, "I never see those on TV or in the papers!" He said that when he came in he was in favor of abortion, but on leaving he was absolutely against it!

Last week a woman asked me for a picture for a meeting of over a thousand kids at her church, and so I gave her the poster I had received from you. (I could use another one!)

Bill O'Brien
Chicago, Illinois

Thank the Good Lord for you—a man of ACTION! While the rest of us were trying to think of something to do about the obscene decision to distribute condoms to high-school children in the New York City schools, you *did* something about it—and not just a plea but a genuine threat that may give them cause to reflect on just what they are getting into. Go get 'em, good Father!

> Joe Scheidler and Staff
> Chicago, Illinois

✠ ✠ ✠ ✠ ✠

The money enclosed is from our son Victor. The kids tithe their earnings each year and then decide where they will send it. Victor's tithe is coming to you.

Please remember him in your prayers. He hopes to find a way to pay for college.

> Melanie Berger
> Indiana

✠ ✠ ✠ ✠ ✠

I hope you have time to read my letter carefully. My husband and I have been fighting this sex-ed mess in Catholic schools since 1968. We have spent twenty-three years in worry and concern over an abomination that should never have been present in our schools. We had virtually no one to help us; parents, by and large, didn't want to "cause waves," "get involved in controversy," etc., and so we went it alone. Priests, too, were obviously unwilling and/or unable to help. So now, twenty-three years later, our own four sons are married and have children of their own, and the sex-ed situation is even worse than ever, preying now on the minds and souls of first-graders.

Believe me, I almost cried to hear my daughter-in-law recently say, "Andrew (first grade, age six) hasn't been wanting to go to Church. We have been encouraging him, hoping it is just a phase he is going through. But the other day he came home from school and said to me that he doesn't like religion class. I asked him to tell me why, and he said, 'I thought the teacher was going to teach me about God, but all she ever talks about is how mommas and daddies make babies.'" I suppose to some people this would be amusing, but to me it is nothing short of tragic. Andrew was sad and disappointed, and it hurts us to think of innocence being replaced with sexual information. I do believe God will truly punish his people for allowing this to happen to our children.

Margery Ferin
West Des Moines, Iowa

✠ ✠ ✠ ✠ ✠

Your Santa Clara conference was the largest, greatest, most inspiring, and most efficiently run conference I have ever attended in my nearly fifty years as a priest. Never before had I been surrounded by so many friendly men and women with doctorate degrees. (And after Father Charles Fiore put a few words of blarney about me on one of the tapes, I tried to avoid having any one of them discover my "feet of clay"!)

I was possibly the last one to leave on Monday,

and the hotel seemed so empty. I missed that spiritual atmosphere generated by all the graced people in attendance and by the presence of the Blessed Sacrament. I'm certain everyone left with renewed inspiration and is eagerly looking forward to next year's conference in Ottawa, Canada.

Father John Clarke
Iowa

✠ ✠ ✠ ✠   ✠

I wish to convey to you my gratitude for your appearance before the state legislature of Louisiana and for the message you delivered to that body. If your admonition is not heeded, it will be because it fell on hardened hearts.

It is beyond my comprehension how a man your age can bear the burdens of your itinerary. We sorely need you. May Our Lord bless you and give you health and strength to continue the great work.

Wilbert J. Gautreaux
Baton Rouge, Louisiana

✠ ✠ ✠ ✠   ✠

It is beyond doubt that *Humanae Vitae* is not the core of teaching evangelized by the bishops and in religious education/formation. Why not? *Humanae Vitae* is a short, precise, and dignified teaching. Since artificial birth control is unacceptable, who needs the details? Certainly not children! Youth will learn everything they want to know about sex that is *negative* from their friends, the media, and on the streets. How can the Church show itself to be pure and holy by getting into the gutter—and dragging children into that gutter—by speaking about the ways and means of contracting AIDS via sodomy; by discussing contraceptive techniques?

I guess some parents want the schools to take over the responsibility of detailed sex education, but the educators should refuse—for the sake of individual children—to do this and should educate the *parents* instead. That's the answer to sex education: Teach the parents how to impart sexual information in a biologically correct and chaste manner.

Anne Stewart Connell
St. Louis, Missouri

✠ ✠ ✠ ✠ ✠

First, let me tell you how much and how often I have thought of you over the past twenty years. We met briefly in California about that long ago when you spoke to a prolife convention. I have kept in touch with a lot of your activities, and I don't know how any human being could give of himself as much as you have. God has to be with you, providing all the energy you need.

For myself, our family is still very active in prolife activities. I still show slides as always, but I do not consider them enough—our people need more of the information that you provide in your many wonderful publications.

Enclosed is my check, which you can put to God's work.

Douglas W. Bel
Bolivar, Missouri

Thank you very much for sending me a copy of *The Flying Monk*.

I certainly want to compliment you on your energetic work in behalf of the unborn. You have made the whole world your ministry, and for this we all owe you a debt of gratitude. Please keep up your fine, important ministry.

> Daniel E. Sheehan
> Archbishop of Omaha
> Omaha, Nebraska

☩ ☩ ☩ ☩ ☩

I pray for you every day at Mass. You deserve our prayers for the great work you do. You have not been shipwrecked, to my knowledge, but otherwise you are the modern Saint Paul. Come to think of it, you've been to many more countries, doing God's work!

> Edward J. Kenney
> Bernardsville, New Jersey

☩ ☩ ☩ ☩ ☩

Your magnificent struggle in the face of death to preserve lives causes me to sense a kinship of my spirit to yours. Reading the report "What Bishops Could Do about Abortion" has been a revelation.

I am sorely troubled at the widespread lack of deep conviction so evident in the leaders that abortion is murder, as truly evil as was the murder of the innocents by Herod. I am troubled that my own heart is not more stirred, is so strangely indifferent, inclined to fatalism, to passive acceptance of this horror that surrounds me, without real heartfelt concern for either the murderers or the murdered.

The least I can do is to give what little I can afford to a brave man who does care, and who proves it over and over. Please pray for me.

> Devillo L. Houck
> Las Cruces, New Mexico

✠ ✠ ✠ ✠ ✠

God bless you, Father Paul. May Mary shield you from the barbs of the brethren, and inspire you to do more and more for our beloved angels dispatched so unceremoniously by our modern pagans.

There is a shortened time now for us all, before the night falls and we go to our rest in Christ Jesus.

> Malachi B. Martin
> New York, New York

✠ ✠ ✠ ✠ ✠

Thank God you are doing something about the sex-education programs in Catholic schools! I am the mother of seven, ages twenty-two down to five. I have always been involved in their schools and feel very strongly that my husband and I are their first and primary teachers.

Unfortunately, as Catholic parents we have been stripped of our rights and duties by the state—and now by Catholic educators. Unless Catholic parents stand up and fight, our children will be lost in the permissive atmosphere of moral relativism permeating the Catholic schools.

Thank God, I am also a former teacher. I am not afraid to take any of them on. We are "glad fools" for Christ.

With God's grace, I recently addressed twenty-five priests and laypeople in education of this great threat to our Catholic family life.

When, oh when, are the bishops going to listen to practicing Catholics who are loyal to the Holy Father?

God bless you, and thanks for allowing me to express some good old-fashioned moral outrage.

> Kathleen Keefe
> Yonkers, New York

✠ ✠ ✠ ✠ ✠

Recently I sent you a check for $10 for some "Freedom of Choice?" postcards. I took a bunch of them to Washington, D.C., last month for the Project II rescues. Many of the rescuers had not seen them! They are a very powerful weapon.

On the second day, I had handed out most of them, and a good number of rescuers were holding them up in front of the clinic as they were being arrested. As I was leaving jail later that day, a black police officer quietly asked me whether he could have one; I gladly obliged.

I have suggested that the bishops should take the money they are going to spend on that public-relations firm and give half of it to you and half to Rescue!

> Richard B. Wilson
> Baldwin, New York

Please send me ten copies each of HLI reprint no. 16 and "IUD: Device of Death." This information is the most concise and best I have seen outside of the medical library in the Carolinas Medical Center, Charlotte, North Carolina.

I plan to share the reprints with other Christians who may not be informed. Many who would not otherwise consider inducing an abortion are, in fact, doing that very thing when they use oral "contraceptives" and the IUD. I especially want our pastor to have this information.

I believe Christian pastors and doctors have a responsibility to inform their congregations of these facts.

Enid C. Hine
North Carolina

✠ ✠ ✠ ✠ ✠

God bless you for your most important work. I am still supporting it, but not financially, because I am having very tough times. You all are present in my daily Mass and rosary.

Please continue to send me extra HLI materials, for I pass them out to anyone who will accept the information. Recently I manned an HLI table at the North Dakota Right to Life convention.

Following daily Mass our parish prays the rosary for the success of HLI activities.

David R. Brien
Grand Forks, North Dakota

Last Saturday morning I received your letter containing the horribly graphic picture of an aborted baby. I am seventy-six years old—too old to be involved very actively—but that day a young woman was helping me with my housework. She is an ardent prolife member of a fundamentalist church. She also works for a doctor who she has heard is an abortionist.

She borrowed the picture and confronted him with it that afternoon. Although he protested that it wasn't real, he appeared to be shaken. His live-in girlfriend was especially shocked.

Here is my check to help with your campaign.

> Dolores Donovan
> Tulsa, Oklahoma

✠ ✠ ✠ ✠   ✠

When Father Paul Marx came to our parish in Greenbelt, Maryland, I was very much impressed. I had expected "fire and brimstone" when our pastor told us who would be preaching, but found instead a gentle but forceful and eloquent speaker. God bless your great work!

> Joan Billerbeck
> Waynesboro, Pennsylvania

✠ ✠ ✠ ✠   ✠

Recently I made my first Holy Communion. A lot of my friends and family came to my party and gave me many nice presents. I got a Bible, two rosaries, a scapular, and money.

I want to give you money to save babies, because I am prolife, too. I have one brother and three sisters, and we love babies. I hope it'll help save babies. I know you do a lot of good work.

Please say a prayer for me and my family to keep us holy.

> Colleen Bodgers
> Holland, Pennsylvania

✠ ✠ ✠ ✠ ✠

Thanks for all you are doing regarding the "Catholic" sex-ed programs. My sister and brother-in-law in Connecticut recently succeeded in having the Benziger family-life series removed from their parish. The new principal couldn't believe all the trash they showed him.

God bless you, and thanks again for your priestly support of parents who are trying to teach their children at home. It means so much to us to know that our faithful priests approve of our attempts to do what we believe to be best for our families and our faith.

> Cathy (Mrs. Bob) Marshall
> Manassas, Virginia

✠ ✠ ✠ ✠ ✠

Please accept my small donation toward your wonderful work. We are living on social security and so our income is small, but a cause such as HLI is one of our main concerns.

As a mother of fifteen children, all grown, my heart aches when I hear of someone aborting a precious life. We raised our family when times were very difficult, but God was with us. It takes faith in God—if only the young people could realize that!

My husband, a convert, and I are in our upper eighties and have 73 grandchildren, 105 great-grandchildren, and 5 great-greats. We love them all.

The world isn't what it was when I was growing up! I'll be remembering you in my prayers.

Margaret Kraft
Durand, Wisconsin

From Yugoslavia

I have been a gynecologist for more than thirty years. Two years ago I gave up doing abortions. Week after week a certain feeling of bitterness had been growing inside me until it became impossible for me to carry on with that sort of activity. It became clear to me that I should not keep on killing people.

So now I have been fighting against abortion, the killing of unborn people. But I have been doing it single-handed, helpless because I have no contact with people who share my opinion. Thank God, I found out about your existence and your combat to save the unborn and preserve the human race by trying to ban legalized abortions.

As far as I know, I am the only gynecologist in Serbia who has refused to do abortions. I estimate that I performed about five abortions daily, which would amount to about 1,500 per year or 45,000 in thirty years. That means I killed the equivalent of a whole good-sized town full of residents.

Please send me your booklets or any sort of

advertising materials and slogans that you print. I hope to be able to gather ideas from them to help in repealing the abortion law of Serbia.

> Dr. Stojan Adasevic
> Belgrade, Yugoslavia

From Zimbabwe

I write initially to thank you for being you and for being such a pillar of strength for all of us involved in the natural ways of fertility management.

Secondly I write in gratitude for materials received from you last week. Our Health Care and Education Office makes fruitful use of all these books by young people as reference books, by students in Bible classes, by users of NFP, and by me as research materials in human-life protection.

Rev. Father Paul Marx, you are dear to me in Bulawayo, for my NFP program virtually exists through you and is rich in resources through you.

> Mrs. S. Gray
> Bulawayo, Zimbabwe

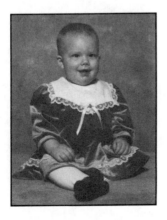

Index